St John's Episcopal Church Edinburgh

Diane M Watters

100 years
Royal
Commission on the
Ancient and
Historical
Monuments of
Scotland

Published in 2008 by The Royal Commission on the Ancient and Historical Monuments of Scotland.

The Royal Commission on the Ancient and Historical Monuments of Scotland (RCAHMS)
John Sinclair House
16 Bernard Terrace, Edinburgh EH8 9NX
tel 0131 662 1456
fax 0131 247 4163
www.rcahms.gov.uk
Registered Charity SC010240

RCAHMS gratefully acknowledges the partnership
support of St John's Episcopal Church, Edinburgh,
which made possible the publication of this volume.

One of Scotland's National Collections, RCAHMS collects, records and interprets information on the architectural, industrial, archaeological and maritime heritage of Scotland. Whether you are working, teaching, studying or simply exploring your local heritage, RCAHMS resources are available to assist your research. You can use our online databases and mapping services to view over 100,000 digital images and to search for information on more than 250,000 buildings or sites, 1.5 million aerial photographs and 2.5 million other photographs, drawings and manuscripts. You can then visit our search room to consult original archive material, Monday to Friday, 9.30am to 4.30pm.

Search our databases online: www.rcahms.gov.uk

Book layout by Mitch Cosgrove
Printed by R R Donnelley, Edinburgh

Front cover: St John's engulfed by the Make Poverty History march on 2 July 2005. © Scotsman Publications

Back cover: 1829 engraving from T H Shepherd's *Modern Athens*, showing Edinburgh's skyline from Craigleith. SC1088556

Contents

Acknowledgements

The concept of an RCAHMS publication devoted to the architectural history of St John's was initiated by Rev. Clephane Hume. She has subsequently carried the project forward with great enthusiasm, and secured support funding. This small publication is the culmination of the ongoing historical research activities begun in the late 1980s by St John's archivist Leslie Hodgson, and the associated 175th anniversary lectures on the history and restoration of St John's in 1993. The research carried out by Leslie Hodgson forms the basis of the factual account of St John's architectural development, and through his expert advice he has made an invaluable contribution to the book. The attempts to set St John's within its wider 19th century architectural, religious, and historical context, has also benefited from the research and advice of a number of individuals, most notably, John Gifford, Miles Glendinning, Aonghus Mackechnie, Allan Maclean, and David Walker. Help was also received from several RCAHMS and St John's colleagues, and other individuals. These included John Armes, Claire Baillie, Oliver Brookes, Tristram Clarke, Jocelyn Cunliffe, Ali Darragh, Tahra Duncan, Lydia Fisher, Ian Fraser, Simon Green, Angus Lamb, Doug MacBeath, Jim Mackie, Anne Martin, Elaine Lee, Angus Mitchell, Miles Oglethorpe, Derek Smart, Tracy Smith, Clare Sorensen, Geoffrey Stell, Jack Stevenson, Ben Tindall, Steve Wallace, and Kristina Watson.

To ease reading, sources have been listed at the end of the main text under Selective Bibliography. All illustrations are Crown Copyright unless otherwise stated. RCAHMS digital reference numbers are given at the end of captions. RCAHMS gratefully acknowledges permission from copyright holders to reproduce illustrations.

Foreword

Sit quietly in St John's on a sunny morning, watch the coloured light from the windows dance on the pillars and you can feel lifted beyond yourself. Stand outside the front door, hear the roar of traffic and the many-accented voices of the crowds passing by, and you feel once again rooted in your humanity. To love God and neighbour is our calling; our building challenges us to do both.

The people who built St John's in 1818 were a self-confident crowd. They were part of the establishment, used to leadership, and were buoyed up by the growing prosperity and military power of the British Empire. We twenty-first century people might have demurred at building on the 'wrong' side of Princes Street, we might have considered it unmannerly to overshadow the much more ancient St Cuthbert's parish church next door, but not they. Though we may be slightly embarrassed to say so now, we cannot help but be grateful to those who chose such a stunning location and who, bit by bit, gave us a building that still inspires and challenges.

Post-Empire and now part of a very different Scotland, the people of St John's in 2008 have our own sense of self-confidence (and no doubt, like our forebears, our own set of self-delusions). Our commitment to walking the way of Jesus Christ encourages us to be a place of welcome, where there is room for all. It encourages us to champion causes of social and international justice and sustainable living, to find partners in mission amongst our Christian neighbours, and to form friendships with those of other faiths. Look beyond the plaques and the memorials to the notice boards, walk down onto the lower terrace, and you will find these priorities expressed in numerous ways.

A church, in short, must always be more than its architecture. Yet, looked at the right way, a building tells a story. In this excellent book, Diane Watters helps us to interpret this story – to understand not only how and when our building came to be but also who shaped it and why they did so. As we at St John's plan a further development of our buildings as a response to God's call to us in a new century, it is instructive to read how those of earlier generations responded to the same call.

I hope you will enjoy reading this architectural guide and that, if you have not already done so, you will visit our church and find it to be not just a beautiful building but a friendly and hospitable place. To us our building is a gift from people we never knew. Please say a prayer for us, so that we in our turn can use this gift well and pass it on with our blessing to the next generation.

**Reverend Dr John Armes, Rector,
St John's Episcopal Church**

Introduction

This is the third book to examine the history of St John's, but the first to record and illustrate its architectural development. In 1911, Rev. George Frederick Terry (rector from 1909–19), compiled his 'little book' *Memorials of the Church of St John the Evangelist, Edinburgh* as a 'pleasing souvenir' for visitors: our 2008 publication has a similar aim. *Memorials* has only a brief section on the architecture of St John's (the author was aided by the church's architect at the time, J M Dick Peddie), and openly admits from the beginning that the neo-Perpendicular style adopted by its architect William Burn, was later viewed by antiquarians and architects alike as a 'debased' one. Terry, who prior to ordination had been an architect, was simply reflecting contemporary early 20th century architectural taste, still greatly influenced by the architectural ideas of the mid-19th century Gothic Revivalist A W N Pugin. Pugin had attacked the 'picturesque eclecticism' of late Georgian architecture, and by the 1840s it was he who claimed that the 15th and early 16th century Perpendicular and Tudor Gothic periods of English architecture were 'debased'. Despite Perpendicular being the most widely used Gothic style in the early phases of the revival (including works by Pugin himself), the impact of his attacks on the neo-Perpendicular were long-lasting, and cast a shadow over the appreciation of early neo-Gothic church design such as that of St John's. In 1926, for example, the young Scottish conservation architect and historian Ian G Lindsay talked of the

2006 view of St John's. DP038454

'depressing Perpendicular' of the 'bad period' in the early decades of the 19th century.

In sharp contrast to these elite architectural views, the broader 19th and 20th century popular image of St John's, as a picturesque architectural monument and place of worship in the heart of Edinburgh, has been repeatedly celebrated in historic views and early photographs. The RCAHMS detailed photographic survey, carried out in 2005–7, is the most recent addition to the visual recording of St John's. This book, of course, touches on the elite architectural debates, and their impact on the design and subsequent alterations at St John's, but crucially, it attempts to re-evaluate its architectural significance and legacy, by considering the broader Scottish religious and cultural impact of the new church building, and its continued central role in the Christian life of Edinburgh's New Town. In the broader cultural sense, this new account owes much to the meticulously researched 1959 *A Short History of the Church of St John the Evangelist* by the historian and St John's vestryman, E W M Balfour-Melville.

A full chronological account of St John's architectural development, illustrated with the rich building archives of RCAHMS, highlights the unique nature of St John's which, despite later additions, stands today much as it was when first designed almost 200 years ago. In 1818, the new chapel of St John's symbolised the spiritual consolidation and tangible recovery of the Scottish Episcopal Church, following its religious and political troubles of the late 17th and 18th centuries. Funded by the wealthy benefactors of the Episcopal church in Edinburgh, St John's played a pivotal

1829 engraving (by W H Bond from a drawing by T H Shepherd) showing St John's and St Cuthbert's Parish Church set against the picturesque backdrop of Edinburgh Castle. From T H Shepherd's Modern Athens. *SC465094*

role in the astonishing nationwide revival of the church in the 19th century. Architecturally, St John's was stylistically advanced, archaeologically 'correct', and its revived neo-Gothic interior was unprecedented in Scotland at that date. It was the first of the Gothic towers and spires that helped create the 'Romantic Edinburgh' cityscape, and enjoyed an enviable backdrop of the castle and Old Town. Its mid-19th century adornment, with pioneering examples of stained glass, and neo-Gothic marble wall monuments providing a narrative of the achievements of the British Empire, enhanced its unique value as an early 19th century Gothic ensemble. Sympathetic and careful extensions in the early 20th century, and sensitive restoration programmes from the 1980s onwards, have upheld and renewed the delicate 19th century aesthetic of St John's, and have safeguarded its significant place – in the words of its former rector, Bishop Neville Chamberlain, in 2003 – as 'one of the great gems of Scottish Architecture.'

View, c.1848, looking west along Princes Street, showing St John's before its new apse was added. SC1077301

2002 view looking west along Princes Street, showing the tower of St John's (furthest to left), which was later joined by those of St George's West (centre), and the triple spires of St Mary's Episcopal Cathedral (right). SC1088522

The Formation of the Congregation

Rev. Daniel Sandford and the Recovery of the
Scottish Episcopal Church in Edinburgh, 1792–1814

The decision to design and build the new Episcopal chapel of St John's, Edinburgh, in late 1814, was a significant one not only for the Bishop of Edinburgh, his clergy and congregation, but for the wider Episcopalian community in early 19th century Edinburgh and Scotland. St John's, along with a small handful of new non-established denominational chapels of high architectural value, symbolised the spiritual consolidation and recovery of the hitherto dwindling Scottish Episcopal Church, following its religious and political troubles of the late 17th and 18th centuries. This recovery led, in turn, to a dramatic revival in the fortunes of the Episcopal Church, and an unprecedented church-building programme in the second half of the 19th century. St John's, Edinburgh, was at the forefront of this movement.

The story of St John's begins in 1792 with the formation of a small Episcopal congregation in rooms in the New Town – composed chiefly of English families residing in Edinburgh – gathered by a young newly-settled Church of England clergyman, Rev. Daniel Sandford (1766–1830). The year 1792 proved to be a significant watershed for the Scottish Episcopal Church. It marked an end to years of religious persecution: the laws which had proscribed Episcopalian worship since 1690 were repealed, and the process of emancipation begun. Only twelve years after this momentous year, and his tentative start as a clergyman, Sandford had risen in 1806 to become the first Englishman to be consecrated as Bishop of Edinburgh in the Scottish Episcopal Church, and his burgeoning congregation had almost outgrown two premises (the latter being the purpose-built Charlotte Chapel of 1797).

1829 mezzotint of Rev. Daniel Sandford, founding rector of St John's and Bishop of Edinburgh, by W Walker and S Cousins.
© *St John's Episcopal Church*

To appreciate the momentous shifts in the fortunes of the Episcopal Church – witnessed in the early 19th century and beyond, in which St John's played a leading role – we must briefly attempt to understand its turbulent past. The history of the Episcopal Church in Scotland since the Reformation of 1560 until the late 18th century is extremely complex, and is closely tied up with the political and religious power struggles during that period. Episcopalianism in Scotland substantially owes its origins to the English Reformation of the 1540s, when the supreme religious authority of the Pope was substituted in England by that of the monarch. The Scottish Reformation rejected Papacy, the mass, and in turn, episcopacy, substituting all these with a Presbyterian system, a church governed not by secular authority but by elected presbyteries and a national 'parliament' of parishes called the General Assembly. The Stuart kings from James VI onwards, however, favoured and pressed for episcopacy, which placed them in charge of the church, and the latter half of the 16th and most of the 17th centuries witnessed tensions between the two systems, which deteriorated intermittently into warfare until the time of forfeiture in 1689. James was replaced as king by William of Orange, his son-in-law, and daughter Mary, and in 1690 Presbyterianism became Scotland's established form of worship. James' supporters, and those of his immediate descendants, tended to be, or were associated with, Episcopalianism (or Catholicism), and were disgruntled by the new settlement. After 1690 the Scottish bishops were not willing to transfer allegiance from the fugitive James to William. All the Scottish bishops who refused to take an oath of allegiance to William and Mary, and the clergy who followed them (known as 'non-jurors' or 'non-swearers') were forced into Episcopal nonconformity.

Because of its loyalty to the Stuart cause in the dynastic wars of the 17th and 18th centuries, the Episcopalian church in Scotland was repressed by the state from the late 17th century until the emancipation in 1792. As part of the 1712 Act of Toleration, Episcopalians who used the liturgy of the Church of England and swore allegiance to Queen Anne, known as 'qualified' clergy and congregations, were tolerated. Because non-jurors could not openly practice, existence of the Episcopal Church relied on 'qualified' chapels with clergymen who had taken the oath of allegiance to the Hanoverian dynasty, but did not give obedience to the Scottish bishops, and were in effect purely congregational.

Not till over a generation had passed after the '45 uprising did the persecution become less severe and the laws more relaxed. The accession of George III in 1760 and death of James VIII (the 'old pretender') in 1766 and of Prince Charles

Edward Stuart in 1788, all eased the pressure on Episcopalians, and by the 1770s it was estimated that there were 1,000 Episcopalians in Edinburgh. Key to our story was the repeal of the late 17th and 18th century laws proscribing Episcopalianism, in 1792, which led ultimately to the reconciliation and union in 1804 of the two sectors of the Episcopal clergy – the former Jacobite 'non-jurors', and the Church of England 'qualified' factions. The leading ecclesiastic behind the repeal of the penal acts in 1792, and the man most responsible for the revival of the Episcopal Church's fortunes at this time, was John Skinner, Bishop of Aberdeen (1744–1816). At an early stage in his long and eventful career, Skinner played a leading role in the negotiations which led to the consecration in 1784 of Samuel Seabury as the first bishop of the Episcopal Church in America. Church of England bishops had refused Seabury consecration because he could not swear allegiance to George III. Skinner's suggestion that the death of Charles in 1788 made it possible for the Episcopal clergy to pray in good conscience for George III, and the Scottish Episcopal Church's acceptance of this argument led to the repeal of the penal acts in 1792, and the union of the two Episcopal factions. In the 1804 convocation at Laurencekirk, the Scottish Episcopal Church adopted the 39 articles of the Church of England and Ireland as its own, and enabled the former 'qualified' clergy to come directly under the authority of the Scottish bishops. In doing so, Skinner effected reconciliation and laid the foundations for a period of consolidation and expansion of the Scottish Episcopal Church in the early 19th century.

The story of St John's begins in 1792 when Sandford, aged only 26, took up an invitation from English Episcopalians in Edinburgh to gather a congregation to worship in rooms at West Register Street. Sandford, born near Dublin and educated at Christ Church Oxford, had moved to Scotland after marrying Helen Frances Catherine, eldest daughter of Erskine Douglas, a 'staunch' Jacobite, in 1790. At first this small 'qualified' congregation did not give obedience to, or come under, the jurisdiction of the then Bishop of Edinburgh, and Sandford, like his fellow English clergymen were independent of any supreme jurisdiction. The growing congregation soon required larger premises and Sandford raised funds to build the new Charlotte Chapel at the

Undated view of the Charlotte Chapel, Rose Street, Edinburgh, opened in 1797 to house Rev. Sandford's growing congregation. By 1814, it was considered too small, and the new church of St John's was proposed. The chapel, purchased by the Baptist Church, was demolished c.1908. © St John's Episcopal Church

memoirs, *Remains of the Late Right Reverend Daniel Sandford*, were published in 1830).

In early 1805, Dr Abernethy Drummond, the Bishop of Edinburgh, retired, and Sandford was consecrated the new bishop in February 1806. This move was strongly supported by Skinner as a means of reconciling the English and Scottish wings of the church. In 1807, at the request of its clergy, the diocese of Fife (i.e. St Andrews) was added to Sandford's jurisdiction and Glasgow followed suit in 1809. During his twenty-four year episcopacy he endeavoured to rebuild diocesan administration, he established six new churches and raised the number of clergy in Edinburgh from seven to twenty-five, and laid the foundations for future growth of the diocese. Throughout this period Sandford retained his congregational charge, but by 1814 his burgeoning congregation had outgrown its premises at the Charlotte Chapel. The chapel was eventually sold to the Baptist Church, who demolished it and built the present Charlotte Street Baptist Chapel on the site in 1908. Sandford now turned his attention to the planning of a grand new church in Princes Street, Edinburgh, that could reflect the raised status and increasing fortunes of the Scottish Episcopal Church. Confidence was not only high within the church, but it was hoped that the end of Britain's period of isolation during the Napoleonic Wars of 1793–1815, was now in sight.

west end of Rose Street which was opened on 28 May 1797. Following the reconciliation of the two Episcopal factions in a union of 1804, Sandford was one of the first English clergymen to place himself, and his Charlotte Chapel congregation, under the jurisdiction of the Scottish bishops when it united to the communion of the Episcopal Church of Scotland on 1 November 1804. Sandford played an important part in the reconciliation of the 'qualified' English clergy with the Scottish Episcopal Church, and wrote an influential pamphlet on the subject in 1804 (his three-volume

The Building of the New St John's, 1814–18

Sir William Forbes of Pitsligo: Funding and Patronage

The project for a new chapel of St John's was initiated in December 1814 when a small group of interested individuals met in Edinburgh's council chambers and resolved that a new and enlarged chapel for Sandford and his congregation should be built. The ways and means of providing a new chapel were initially open to discussion. On 31 May 1815, Sandford approached the Rev. Archibald Alison (1757–1839) and his former 'qualified' congregation at the Cowgate Chapel in the Old Town, and suggested an ambitious joint chapel-building venture. The two merged congregations should, according to Sandford, 'build one magnificent church': apparently the site of this new proto-Episcopal cathedral was to be at the foot of The Mound, where the medieval Old Town faced the classical New Town. This idea was soon abandoned as the size of the merged congregations was believed to be too large, and it was considered that two new chapels at the east and west end of the New Town would be more practical. Both congregations agreed that donations from England towards the new church-buildings should be equally divided between them. Almost immediately the two separate Episcopal congregations pressed ahead with their own plans. The foundations of the new St Paul's Episcopal Chapel, York Place

Portrait of Sir William Forbes of Pitsligo, by Sir Henry Raeburn, 1823. Forbes was the lead trustee and patron of St John's. © The Governor and Company of the Bank of Scotland

(designed by Archibald Elliot), were laid in April 1816, and it was built in parallel with St John's. It was consecrated and opened by Bishop Sandford just two months before St John's, in January 1818. The histories of the two new chapels, as we will see, remained inextricably linked through patronage, personal connections, and ultimately through the mutual aspirations of the two Episcopal congregations.

1815 engraving (by D Somerville) of a perspective view of Burn's seven-bay proposal for St John's, showing the original design for the tower. During construction in January 1818, the tower was severely storm-damaged, and was quickly replaced by a more orthodox tower design. © Duke of Buccleuch and Queensberry. SC1077278

In June 1815, a committee of seven close-knit and influential trustees from the existing Charlotte Chapel congregation, including Sandford, was established and entrusted to raise funds (£18,000), purchase the chosen site at the west end of Princes Street, then a market garden, and oversee the entire project. The lead trustee was the prominent banker, Sir William Forbes of Pitsligo, assisted chiefly by Colin Mackenzie of Portmore (d.1830), deputy keeper of the Signet, and James Clerk (d.1831), a judge at the Exchequer Court. The largest subscribers to the share issue were: Forbes (the major shareholder); Charles William Henry Scott, the fourth Duke of Buccleuch; Archibald John Primrose, the Earl of Rosebery (a politician who was the patron of the neo-Gothic Dalmeny House, West Lothian, designed by William Wilkins, 1814–17); William Kerr, sixth Marquis of Lothian; and James Clerk. Those individuals represented the wealthy elite benefactors of the unified Episcopal Church in early 19th century Edinburgh. A glance at those involved in the early history of St John's uncovers a web of financial, cultural, religious, and personal connections – including the young architect William Burn – out of which emerges a fascinating insight into the social structure of the church in the early 19th century.

The key figure, William Forbes, was the eldest son of an influential banker and benefactor of the same name who had been raised by his young widowed mother, Christian Forbes, in the Episcopal faith. His own father had had strong Jacobite connections. Forbes the elder attended the 'qualified' Episcopal chapel in Blackfriars Wynd, and led a group of influential patrons who engineered and funded the new Cowgate Chapel – designed 1772–4 in the classical style by John Baxter the younger. In 1800 he personally secured the services of Rev. Archibald Alison to lead the congregation of the Cowgate Chapel. The role of enlightened church benefactor was carried energetically forward by his eldest son, William, following his father's death in 1806. In the early decades of the 19th century – during the formative years of Forbes the younger's career – the plethora of banking companies in Glasgow and Edinburgh became increasingly unsustainable, and many were forced to merge. Forbes, Hunter & Co. merged with the Glasgow Union Bank and The Ship Bank in 1838, and in turn was totally absorbed in 1843 to form the Union Bank of Scotland. In 1955 that bank was merged with the Bank of Scotland. William's younger brother, John Hay Forbes (later Lord Medwyn, 1776–1854), was also a leading layman in the Scottish Episcopal Church and was instrumental in the formation of the new St Paul's Episcopal Chapel, York Place, and one of its benefactors. The family tradition of involvement with the Scottish Episcopal Church reached its 19th century peak when John Forbes' eldest son, Alexander Penrose Forbes (1817–1875), became Bishop of Brechin in 1847, while his second son, George Hay Forbes (1821–75) also became an Episcopal clergyman and scholar.

Like his father, William Forbes had wide social connections outside the world of banking. He became a lifelong friend of Sir Walter Scott, despite his having beaten Scott in 1795 to the hand of Williamina Belsches Stuart, hailed by Scott as his 'first love'. Forbes' firm, Sir William Forbes & Co., adopted a shield and stag motto which came from Scott's epitaph for Forbes the elder which contained the line 'The widow's shield, the orphan's stag'. Although Scott was not a particularly religious man, his associations with St John's are notable: he buried his 'dear mother' in St John's eastern enclosed burial ground on 29 December 1819, and reportedly had a pew in his name within the church, occupied by his wife, Charlotte Carpenter.

William Burn's Design

From the very beginning, Forbes directed and oversaw all elements of the new chapel project, and began a long close relationship between St John's and the Forbes family. Forbes first entered into discussions with the prominent architect James Gillespie (1777–1855) in August 1815. In May 1815, Gillespie married the heiress Margaret Anne Graham, daughter of William Graham of Orchill, and entered the Episcopalian gentry (renaming himself James Gillespie Graham in the 1820s), and he would probably have become known to Forbes. Gillespie Graham, who relished the idea of a 'further specimen of the Gothic in our Capital', had designed and built the new Catholic chapel in Picardy Place, Edinburgh, in 1813–14, and began in 1814 his ambitious Gothic Oxbridge college chapel-fronted St Andrew's Catholic Church, Glasgow (later Cathedral). In 1815 Gillespie

1987 view of the influential neo-Gothic St Andrew's Catholic Cathedral, Clyde Street, Glasgow, designed in 1814 by J Gillespie Graham. In 1815, Graham was approached to design St John's, but was soon dropped in favour of William Burn. SC1077279

Graham's career as a fully-fledged architect was developing: his status in the early years appears to have been that of a clerk of works-come-architect, but by 1810 he had several large commissions underway. Gillespie Graham specialised in Gothic churches and neo-medieval castellated country houses. His greatest achievement in religious design was the towering Gothic Victoria Hall, Edinburgh, of 1839–44, where he was ably assisted by his friend, the young English architect A W N Pugin (1812–52), who was soon to become the most influential figure in the mid-19th century Gothic Revival in England (see below). In a short period of time, however, the professional relationship between Gillespie Graham and Forbes over the new St John's collapsed. Gillespie Graham's first proposal was for a small aisle-less chapel (similar to the 1813 design for Collace Church, Perthshire, attributed to him), but he was immediately informed by Forbes that although the breadth of the chapel was limited (60 feet wide), a nave and side aisles were 'indispensable'. The altered designs, penned by Gillespie Graham's staff, were, through some 'unaccountable mistake' sent to the trustees un-checked by Gillespie Graham himself. Despite an apology from Gillespie Graham, and new updated plans being sent in early August 1815, Forbes

did not continue with his architectural services. A dispute over payment between Gillespie Graham and Forbes ensued, which lasted over five years, and arbitration was finally agreed in August 1820.

As relations with Gillespie Graham disintegrated, a successful partnership between Forbes and the young architect William Burn (1789–1870), recently returned to his native Edinburgh from London, was established. Correspondence between the two men began in July 1815. Burn's letters of business with Forbes (held in the Fettercairn Papers in the National Library of Scotland) contrast starkly with the slightly older Gillespie Graham's short, hasty scrawls. From the beginning, Burn methodically and precisely detailed what had been authorised by the trustees, his own responsibilities of design and supervision of works, and, of course, his fees: an agreed 5% fee of the overall building costs. The early decades of the 19th century were a transitional period for the architectural world: architecture had ceased to be a trade, but had not yet become a profession. In 1834 the Institute of British Architects was formed (Burn was one of its earliest members), and by the 1840s architecture became

Daguerreotype, c.1840, of William Burn, architect of St John's, 1815–8. © Madras College, St Andrews. SC1077292

firmly established as a recognisable profession with corresponding standards of professional conduct and remuneration. From the very beginning Forbes was clearly impressed with Burn's architectural talent and business-like approach, and in 1826 he commissioned Burn to reconstruct his own house, Fettercairn, Kincardineshire, in the neo-Jacobean style.

William Burn was born in Edinburgh on 20 December 1789, the fourth child of Robert Burn (1751–1815), architect, builder and minor landowner. William initially trained as an architect with his father, who had a good practice in medium-sized country houses and in Edinburgh was responsible for the development of the lands of Picardy (including Picardy Place, Forth Street, Union Street and Broughton Street), and the Nelson Monument on Calton Hill in 1807. In 1808 William obtained a pupilage in Sir Robert Smirke's office in London. Smirke (1780–1867), a committed Greek Revivalist, created one of the biggest and most commercially successful architectural practices of 19th century London.

In 1811, Burn returned to Scotland as site architect for Smirke's cubic neo-Grecian Kinmount House, Dumfriesshire, and subsequently established his own architectural practice – first from the family building yard in Leith, and then in 1814, from an office in George Street. Building activity in the capital was at a low ebb due to the practical and economic impact of the Napoleonic Wars, but Burn secured an important commission in 1813 with his impressive Greek Revival design for the large new North Leith Parish Church, Edinburgh. As a landowner in the parish, his father was an active heritor, and was instrumental in getting his son this key early commission. In the early decades of the 19th century neo-Classicism was firmly established in Edinburgh's New Town. The ascendancy of the Greek revival had, by the 1820s, won the capital its reputation as the *Athens of the North*. The majority of Burn's earliest public commissions displayed the Greek purity and logic that he had been exposed to in Smirke's office. By 1815, as he was finalising his designs for St John's, Burn was still at the very beginning of a highly successful career. He was one of a group of 'bright young' architects newly returned to Scotland from London at that time, who came to dominate the Scottish architectural scene, displacing and ultimately superseding the

older David Hamilton in Glasgow, and Gillespie Graham in Edinburgh. In church building terms, St John's was the first of Burn's large neo-Gothic commissions, and was to lead to the first of his often controversial and radical restorations and rebuilding of ecclesiastical monuments at Dunfermline Abbey Kirk in 1818–21, followed by the re-facing of St Giles in 1829–32. A handful of key domestic commissions in the 1820s soon snowballed into a prolific country house practice in the 1830s and 40s, unparalleled in 19th century Scotland. He revolutionised large-scale domestic planning in country house architecture, and soon broke into the English market. Burn set up office in London in 1844 (leaving his partner David Bryce in charge of the Edinburgh office), and became the celebrated architect of the Tory landed gentry.

By late August 1815, Burn's final design for the 'new English chapel' of St John had been approved by Forbes and the Trustees. The site for the chapel was clearly limited, and the brief taxing: the site of the former market garden sloped steeply away to the south, and the breadth of the chapel, which would run parallel to Princes Street, should accommodate 800 people, be Gothic in style, and consist of nave and aisles. Outweighing these limitations, however, was the unique and picturesque character of the site: it was the sole building occupying the east

Detail of Kirkwood's Plans and Illustrations of the City of Edinburgh, *plates 4 & 5, 1817, showing the former Charlotte Chapel, Rose Street, and the outline of the new St John's Chapel, Princes Street, which was under construction at the time. DP018427*

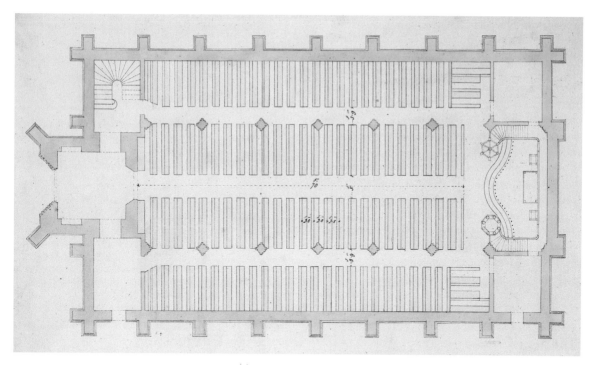

Ground floor plan, c.1817, of St John's as built (unattributed), showing position of pews. SC836059

end of the southern side of the New Town's most prestigious linear street, and had as its setting the visually dramatic backdrop of Edinburgh's rugged castle rock and the silhouetted ridge of the Old Town. Tucked behind, and at a lower level to the south, was St Cuthbert's Parish Church. Originally a medieval religious site, it was reconstructed in 1773–5 by the builder-architect James Weir of Tollcross, with a steeple by Alexander Stevens of 1789–90. With the addition of St John's, a 'holy-corner' – a cluster of religious buildings common in 19th century Edinburgh – was begun at the foot of Lothian Road. According to St John's historian, E W M Balfour-Melville, Walter Scott is reputed to have described the neighbouring church of St Cuthbert's as 'the box which St John's came in'.

Burn's approved design had three enforced changes during construction: the addition of an extra bay, a new tower, and the planned addition of an enclosed eastern burial ground abutting the east end of the church. Despite 19th and 20th century internal alterations, and one significant addition (a new chancel), St John's today remains substantially as it was when first designed: a fact that clearly adds to its architectural value. Burn designed an English

neo-Gothic (Perpendicular style) rectangular basilica-plan church with a raised central nave – lit by clearstory windows – and two flanking lower aisles. Constructed of polished sandstone (from the Red Hall quarry, Edinburgh), it had a flat east end with a six-light window surmounted by a wheel window of radiating tracery, and a tall square single-windowed belfry tower at the other end (which contained the west entrance), topped by pinnacles and an octagonal open stone lantern. Originally the side elevations consisted of seven bays with buttresses and pinnacles, and the eastern and westernmost end bays had elaborately corbelled niches instead of the existing large rectilinear-traceried windows.

In March 1816, the building contractors David MacGibbon and James Ritchie commenced the foundations. At this stage the first change to Burn's original plan was made. The addition of an extra bay did not, it could be argued, significantly change the external proportions of the church, but this decision had a profound impact on the visual strength of the church's interior space. Forbes and the trustees became convinced that the new chapel would seem square in plan, and would appear too squat, like contemporary centralised Presbyterian preaching-box kirks. As a result it would lack the processional and rectilinear character of a suitably neo-Gothic church. The new chapel was originally to seat 800 people in the nave, aisles and proposed surrounding gallery. This anticipated a 30–35% growth in the congregation. When the extra bay was added, it was also agreed to reduce the seating to 700 (a more realistic aspiration for the new congregation), omit all but the small organ gallery at the west end, and accommodate the lost gallery seating in the extra bay. With the encircling gallery omitted, the appearance of Burn's magnificent interior remained visually uninterrupted. The nave was separated from the tall arcades of the north and south aisles by slender columns of clustered shafts – each pier ending with a leaning-out figure of the pentinent Magdalene as a label-stop. Thin clearstorey wall-shafts ran up and erupted into decorative plaster fan-vaults, abutting the central fans (of the same diameter) with delicate dramatic hanging pendants. The chancel was housed behind the broad arch over the nave, in the flat-ended shallow easternmost bay, lit by the large east window. North of the chancel

Engraving (by B Howlett, 1812) of St Botolph's Church, Boston, Lincolnshire, showing its 15th century tower – a possible source for Burn's original tower at St John's. From John Britton's Architectural Antiquities of Great Britain, *published 1805–14. DP030510*

Engraving by J and H S Storer, c.1820, showing St John's newly built, but without its south terrace and eastern walled burial ground, from Storer and Storer's Views in Edinburgh and its vicinity, exhibiting remains of antiquity, public buildings and picturesque scenery, *published 1820. DP029333*

was the vestry, and to the south a porch with an opening on to the terrace.

Construction progressed steadily for almost two years, but Burn's design suffered a setback when the partly completed tower was damaged by a severe storm which raged over Edinburgh in mid-January in 1818. The *Edinburgh Evening Courant* reported that on 15 January at 'half past four, the turrets and other ornaments upon the tower of Bishop Sandford's elegant new Chapel, at the west end of Princes Street, were blown down with a dreadful force', and two days later it recorded that 'the builder appears to have taken every proper precaution to secure the work by copper bolts but the violence of the gale was irresistible, the metal was drawn from its sockets, the stone broken to pieces, and several large masses, weighing from four to five hundredweight, were carried by the current of wind, and fell at an angle of about forty degrees'.

In a letter of 17 January 1818, Walter Scott gave his account of the dramatic events: 'We have had dreadful weather here, all the gothic pinnacles on the new Episcopal Chapel are blown down, and have fallen on the roof and forced their way into the body of the building so that the horns of the Bishop's mitre have got into the guts of the church'. Burn's original tower and octagonal stone lantern used as its source the famous lofty tower of one of England's largest Gothic parish churches, St Botolph, Boston, Lincolnshire (tower begun

1425–30 and completed *c.*1520), but Burn may also have been aware of the similar tower design by Thomas Harrison at St Nicholas, Liverpool, 1811–15. The replacement tower (which we see today), completed only nine weeks following the collapse of its predecessor, provided a more conventional 'in-keeping' neo-Perpendicular double-windowed belfry tower with simple pinnacled top, as seen in the numerous attached towers of English parish churches. Other possible sources may have been the 15th century towers of York Minster and the high twin towers of Beverley Minster.

Running parallel to this rebuilding, as part of a separate venture privately funded by Forbes, Mackenzie and Clerk, but to Burn's original design, the newly-created platform upon which the chapel sat was extended to the south to form a walled terrace over a lower cloistered burial area of seventeen arcades. In addition, the ground at the east end of the church – beyond the flat-ended chancel area – was laid out as a small burying

Lithograph, c.1845, (drawn by W Mason from a daguerreotype), showing the south front of St John's from Castle Terrace. DP030519

ground surrounded by a high stone wall (single storey, of five bays, with a canted end) and gates – known later as the dormitory. Further building on the site was, from the outset, very restricted. Since 1801, owners of properties on the north side of Princes Street had been in legal wrangles with the Town Council over feuing, for building purposes, of the grounds on the south side of Princes Street. Opposition to further building was galvanised by the construction of St John's, and in 1816 a private Act of Parliament, which prohibited the erection of any further buildings on the south side of Princes Street, from The Mound to Lothian Road, secured the proprietors' open view of the castle. The land, feued by the Princes Street proprietors from the Town Council under the 1816 Act, was laid out to form West Princes Street Gardens: a private garden designed by James Skene of Rubislaw (1755–1864), with Robert Stevenson as engineer. After twenty-one years at the Charlotte Chapel, Bishop Sandford preached his last sermon there on Sunday 15 March 1818. The new St John's was consecrated on 19 March and opened for divine service on Good Friday, 20 March 1818.

Front cover of the history and abstract accounts of St John's, 1815–37. The volume was bound by Robert Seton, Edinburgh. © The National Archives of Scotland

The Gothic Style

The Architectural and Ecclesiastical Context of St John's

St John's and the Early 19th Century Neo-Gothic

Why was the new 'English chapel' designed in the neo-Perpendicular Gothic style? What ecclesiastical Gothic architectural sources and contemporary examples did Burn draw upon when designing St John's, and how typical a design was it? And in turn, what religious meaning did this style signify to its Episcopalian congregation in Edinburgh? The context of 19th century architectural revivalism, and in particular the neo-Gothic, must be briefly examined in order to answer these questions.

The style that dominated early 19th century architecture had been the Classical, based on the revival of Greek and Roman antiquity, which was re-introduced into the British Isles in the wake of the Italian Renaissance – at which time the Gothic style was rejected as irregular and irrational. The crucial change in attitudes to style came in the middle-to-late 18th century, when scholars and historians overturned the rigid idea that only Classical antiquity was worthy of study, and they began to take an interest in the wider variety of forms surviving from the past. A parallel development was the breakdown of the established rules of artistic or architectural value. Through the development of the aesthetics of the Picturesque and Sublime in the late 18th century, art and architecture which did not adhere to the strict rules of beauty, could now be appreciated for the reactions and images they could evoke: in particular, Gothic could be appreciated for its surprise, irregularity, and exaggerated forms, and eventually for its emotive ability to conjure up romantic images and thoughts of a medieval past long gone.

Initially, Gothic was exploited for its suggestive quality of decay and melancholy, when mock Gothic ruins were placed in the 18th century Picturesque landscape gardens of England. But this scenographic, light-hearted, and often politically naive use of Gothic was soon overturned in the early decades of the 19th century as significant developments in architectural history were made by a number of English antiquarians and architects. Key amongst the antiquarians were John Britton, John Milner and Thomas Rickman, who established a more specialist understanding of England's rich Gothic heritage through extensive study and recording (Scotland's medieval antiquarian study was to come later). Through their work a growing corpus of publications for contemporary architects to draw upon became available. John Britton published in 1805–14 his lavishly illustrated *Architectural Antiquities of Great Britain*. Milner's *Treatise on the Ecclesiastical Architecture of England during the Middle Ages* of 1811, and Rickman's *Attempt to Discriminate the Styles of English Architecture* of 1819, both began the formal classification of Gothic by establishing historical developments of the style in England. Rickman's publication became a practical handbook, and enabled architects to work consciously in a 'correct' style throughout their building. The detailed study of England's medieval churches and monasteries by specialist church architects, like Rickman, and by religious antiquarians, forged a strong link between Gothic and ecclesiastical architecture in the early 19th century. This bond became inseparable in the fully-blown Victorian Gothic Revival led by the influential polemicist and architect A W N Pugin.

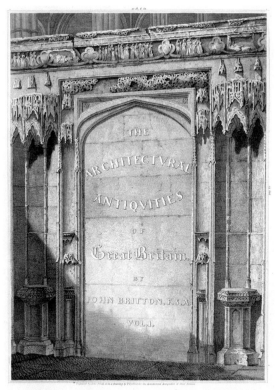

Frontispiece engraving (by J Smith from a drawing by P Gyfferd, 1807, showing part of the screen in Edward the Confessor's Chapel, Westminster Abbey, London) of John Britton's highly-influential antiquarian study Architectural Antiquities of Great Britain *(Volume I), from 1835 edition. DP030511*

The Perpendicular exterior forms and decorative detailing of St John's sat firmly within the English early 19th century neo-Gothic context, but in fact St John's was stylistically somewhat 'advanced' compared to its contemporaries in England. Burn showed a sophisticated understanding of the stylistic unity of Perpendicular: his lofty nave, shouldered between two lower aisles, tall arcading, slender piers, and fan-vaulted ceiling were unprecedented not only in Scotland, but in English Gothic revivalism. The neo-Perpendicular, which was almost universally adopted by church architects in England in the early decades of the 19th century, was based on the idiosyncratic late-medieval Gothic of England, characterised by a formal rectangular geometry, low, four-centred arches, and hoodmoulds. Utilising lead as a roof covering, which allowed roofs to be almost flat, fully-fledged Perpendicular provided higher walls to compensate for loss of height from steeply pitched roofs. These lofty walls were filled with large areas of rectangular traceried glass, interspersed by buttresses in the manner of the early 16th century King's College Chapel, Cambridge. The introduction of highly decorative stone fan vaulting was one of Perpendicular's greatest visual and technical achievements: the early 16th century ceilings at St George's Chapel, Windsor, King Henry VII's Chapel, Westminster, and the fan vaulted ceiling at King's College (1512–15) were key Perpendicular sources for St John's architectural decoration.

The popularity of the Perpendicular as a revived style has been attributed to its orderliness, emphasis on vertical linearity, strong delineated borders of its rectangular patterning, and elegant high naves. Its grid-like decoration could be easily used as a Gothic cladding for large barn-like modern church interiors. The main early 19th century architect to use the neo-Perpendicular in England, Thomas Rickman, adopted an archaeologically 'correct' style for the exteriors of his early churches, but his interiors were modern galleried spaces for large congregations. It was not until the 1820s that attempts were made to revive the interior stylistic qualities of Gothic such as at St Luke's, Chelsea (1820–4, by John Savage), with its pioneering stone-vaulted ceiling and slender flying buttresses. So Burn's design of 1815 was unusual in being stylistically 'correct' throughout: an early example of basilican neo-Gothic at a time when scholarly knowledge of Gothic was in its infancy. St John's vaulted ceiling was of course constructed of wood and plaster, not stone, and its original east window was surmounted by a wheel window of radiating tracery – not a recognised neo-Perpendicular element. The specific original sources were clearly the 16th century English Perpendicular masterpieces. But these notable English late-Gothic collegiate chapels had vast flat-ended Perpendicular windows at east and west ends – a formula adopted by Gillespie Graham at the Catholic St Andrew's chapel in Glasgow. Burn clearly looked to both the English parish church and traditional Scottish medieval and post-medieval church formulas, with large axial towers on their entrance fronts, when designing St John's. In the first few decades of the 19th century the entrance tower or steeple was a common feature in Scottish church architecture.

Contemporary examples included Kincardine in Menteith Parish Church of 1814–16 by Richard Crichton, and David Hamilton's later Campsie High Church, Lennoxtown (1827–8).

Why was a Scottish Gothic architectural source not used at St John's? Firstly, an architect designing in a 19th century revivalist style, like Burn, would have drawn on published architectural sources but, by 1815, there were no significant antiquarian studies of Scotland's medieval architecture. It was not until the publication in 1845–52 of Robert Billings' *Baronial and Ecclesiastical Antiquities of Scotland* that a reliable visual source book was actually available to Scottish revivalist architects. This beautifully produced publication, co-written and fully illustrated by the English architect and Gothic enthusiast Billings, was part-funded by William Burn, who apparently sought out Billings in London and advanced him £1,000 as an inducement to undertake the mammoth task of providing what would become the prototypal and invaluable source book and visual quarry for the Scotch Baronial style in the latter half of the 19th century. The three-volume *Ecclesiastical Architecture of Scotland* by MacGibbon and Ross was published in 1896–7. Despite the importance of these publications, however, they were not complemented by a detailed chronological framework for Scottish medieval architecture, such as that developed in larger European countries, and in particular 19th century England and France.

On the whole, medieval Scottish architecture had followed a different course from that of England, France and northern Europe: the dominant late medieval heritage of Scotland, was, of course, its grand castles and palaces, which were abundantly 'revived' between the mid-18th and the early 20th century. However, Scotland could boast a small but prestigious ecclesiastical Gothic heritage: the late Gothic building programme of the second half of the 13th century, built prior to the 14th century Wars of Independence, was witnessed at Glasgow Cathedral (13th century choir, crypt, chapter house and transepts), and Elgin Cathedral (re-building after the fire of 1270), and in the 15th century at St Michael's, Linlithgow (1480–90), and the *c.*1500 crown steeple of St Giles, Edinburgh. But the influence of medieval Gothic as an international style for the great churches of Europe was, on the whole, little felt in Scotland. Warfare

and the Scottish Reformation of 1560 contributed to the destruction and neglect of medieval buildings. In Presbyterian worship there was no need for long-naved processional Gothic churches, and those that were taken over by the new Reformed church were often much altered and sub-divided to meet the requirements of the new form of worship. Gothic, on the whole, had far less emotional and historical resonance in the centuries that followed the 16th century, and the Gothic survival that characterised English architecture until the fully-blown 19th century revival was almost absent in Scotland.

Subsequently, any early attempt at reviving a Scottish Gothic had to start from a low base and contrasted significantly with the vast Gothic church building stock of England. Historical revivalism in Scotland, because of this and a number of other important factors, as we will see, took a very different course from that of 18th and 19th century England. In the late 18th century a number of isolated yet advanced attempts at revived Gothic in Scotland began, including James Playfair's Farnell Church, Angus, of 1789, and Craig Church, Angus, 1797–9, by Richard Crichton. But it was not until Gillespie Graham's neo-Gothic chapels (Perpendicular and Decorated) for the Catholic Church, and Archibald Elliot's and Burn's equivalents for the Episcopal Church in the second decade of the 19th century that the 'problem' of adapting Gothic to preaching-orientated Presbyterian worship could be put aside, and a fully integrated Gothic formula for church building with sophisticated decoration and long plan-form could be pursued.

1829 engraving (by W Watkin from a drawing by T H Shepherd), of St Paul's Episcopal Church, York Place, from T H Shepherd's Modern Athens. *St Paul's, was designed by Archibald Elliot, and built in parallel with St John's. DP029337*

View, c.1880, showing Princes Street and its gardens from the Mound, by G Washington Wilson. St John's (in the distance, centrally placed), still has its flat east end. SC1082781

Whilst the early 19th century neo-Perpendicular Gothic adopted at the new chapel of St John's was characterised by a regular and dignified reticence (a virtue that enabled it to fit politely into the neo-Classical ensemble of Edinburgh's New Town), the importance of its unique and rugged picturesque landscape setting, as an inspiration to Burn, has perhaps been overlooked. In much early 19th century neo-Gothic work, considerations of harmony, irregularity, movement and contrast, were still purposefully and consciously evoked. A leading protagonist of this approach was the architect and gifted draughtsman, Thomas Sandby (1723–98). Although little of his architectural work has survived, his drawings focus on the relationship between architecture and landscape, integrating restrained neo-Gothic churches and their landscapes into a seamless ensemble. Sandby's atmospheric *c.*1790 drawing of an unidentified church (in the Architectural Archives of the University of Pennsylvania) provides a fine example of this approach: a slender church not dissimilar to St John's is set at the base of a mountainous rock-formation strikingly similar to Arthur's Seat, Edinburgh. The church's spiky and jagged outline is set carefully within the composition to both contrast and harmonise with its setting. Similarly, viewed from the westernmost entrance to Princes Street, St John's silhouette of delicate spiky Gothic pinnacles contrasted starkly with its visual backdrop of the heavy, rugged castle rock, and, of course, its neo-Classical neighbours. Until the late 1830s, St John's was the only prominent neo-Gothic building in the heart of Edinburgh's cityscape.

What religious meaning did a revived English Perpendicular neo-Gothic style signify to its congregation and the people of Edinburgh in the early 19th century? The survival and revival of Gothic as a style in England, unlike Scotland, had strong emotive cultural, religious and political resonance, and was linked to notions of national

1829 engraving (by W Tombleson from a drawing by T H Shepherd) showing Edinburgh's skyline from Craigleith. St John's, to the right of the dome of St George's, Charlotte Square, has the enviable backdrop of the dramatic castle rock. From T H Shepherd's Modern Athens. *DP029336*

identity. In England, the support of the Gothic, as opposed to the Classical style, was strongest amongst the traditionally conservative institutions of the nobility, church and universities, who for various reasons harked back to the medieval landscape of England. Some of the greatest Perpendicular late-Gothic monuments were associated with these institutions, and the choice of this style may, in the minds of Burn and his clients, have helped raise the status of the new St John's above the role of a mere English parish church. For the strong émigré English element of St John's congregation, including its bishop, it may possibly have evoked similar notions of tradition, legitimacy, and ecclesiastical status. The appointment of Sandford as the new Bishop of Edinburgh in 1806 – following the reconciliation and union in 1804 of the two sectors of the Episcopal clergy – aimed to placate the discontented English 'side' in the early days of the union. The adoption of an English revived style for St John's supports this theory. The history of the Episcopal Church in Scotland in the 18th and 19th centuries was closely tied up with its relationship to its sister church in England: St John's, it could be argued, was a legitimate architectural embodiment of this close relationship in the early 19th century following the union – although of course, as the 19th century progressed, Gothic became increasingly linked with Anglican revival in England, and in turn was viewed as 'Popish' by many in Scotland (including architects such as Alexander Thomson).

The Legacy of St John's and the Mid-19th Century Gothic Revival

What architectural and ecclesiastical legacy, if any, did St John's leave in the capital? This is a difficult question to answer, as an authoritative and detailed survey of 19th century historical revivalism in Scottish architecture has yet to be carried out, but some tentative conclusions can be attempted. The neo-Gothic was in its infancy in early 19th century Scotland, and St John's heralded a heightened level of scholarship and stylistic correlation between interior and exterior forms in church design. This scholarship was fundamentally modelled on English architectural developments. In England, however, the neo-Gothic movement was in the course of further radical change. By the

early Victorian decades of the 1830s and 40s two key forces were changing it from a stylistic revival with associational values, to an ideological and religious cultural movement which used the culture of the medieval period as a benchmark to judge contemporary 19th century culture. The Tractarian revival (or Oxford Movement) reinvigorated Anglican worship: it emphasised the fundamentals of the Christian church, focused on spirituality and ritual, and harked back to a medieval golden age. Running parallel to this was the greatly influential architectural and ecclesiological polemic of Pugin, as shown in his 1836 publication *Contrasts*. Pugin attacked the culturally materialistic and mechanistic products of modern Enlightenment utilitarianism as witnessed in the 18th and early 19th centuries. He stressed the need to return to 'honest' expression of forms, and found the answer – in terms of church design – in the 'truthfulness' of the Early and Decorated styles of English architecture of the 13th and early 14th centuries. For Pugin and his many followers, the medieval church, in terms of plan (with deep chancel) and 'high' church liturgy, and reliance on the decorative arts, was an expression of the true faith, and crucially brought with it the sought-after medieval mysteriousness, for which all Gothic revivalists hankered. These influences subsequently swept through the Church of England.

All this, of course, had little impact on St John's, as this seismic change took place after its completion, but crucially, it did directly shape mid-late 19th century views of Anglican church architecture, and resulted in its most significant alteration – the addition of a deep chancel in 1882 (see below). The early neo-Gothic, which St John's epitomised, came directly under attack from Pugin and his followers as much as non-Gothic post-Enlightenment architecture. Anticipating this trend perhaps, Thomas Rickman criticised St John's for its 'constant repetition of small parts', despite his own neo-Perpendicular and Decorated style churches displaying strikingly similar thin tracery such as St David's (Ramshorn) Church, Glasgow, of 1824–6. The early 19th century neo-Gothic style, with its symmetrical plan form and no prominent chancel, was the antithesis of Pugin's medieval vision of moral architecture, where the diverse functions of a building were clearly expressed by its exterior form.

Ultimately this search for architectural fundamentals led Pugin and his followers to argue that Gothic, as an honest expression of a building's function, was not just a fanciful style, but could be rationally applied to all types of 19th century buildings. Although St John's heralded a new level of revived Gothic in early 19th century Scotland, it was a style primarily used for church buildings, and to a lesser extent monuments, and the potency and all-encompassing nature of the Gothic Revival, with its strong English cultural roots, did not become a British-wide phenomenon. The Gothic Revival, however, did have a significant impact on one key Scottish institution: the Scottish Episcopal Church. St John's and its contemporaries forged strong links between the revitalised non-established faith, and the neo-Gothic style. In turn, the strong links between the Scottish Episcopal Church and the Church of England further strengthened these cultural and religious ties in architectural design. In fact, the Tractarian movement, as recent historians of the Scottish Episcopal Church have highlighted, revered the Scottish church as one which had maintained its pre-Reformation theology, was non-established, free from state intervention, and, like the medieval church, had a history of persecution. And in the event, most church designs in the Scottish Episcopal Church building drive of 1842–59 came to conform to the principles argued by Pugin, the Tractarian movement, and the later, highly-influential, Ecclesiological Society.

The Ecclesiological Society, founded in 1845 when the 1836 Cambridge Camden Society was re-named, began life as a typical local antiquarian and archaeological society. But from 1841 it produced a flourish of new publications and pamphlets which provided directions for the proper and accepted church building formulas promoted by Pugin, and acted as a governing moral critique of new designs: *The Ecclesiologist* became one of the most important and influential English architectural periodicals of the mid-19th century. Although some Scottish architects, notably the favoured Scottish Episcopal Church architect John Henderson, achieved competence in 'correct' Gothic Revival design, the church usually employed key English architects for their most prestigious works (excluding Henderson's Trinity College, Glenalmond, 1841–51, of which Rev. Bannerman Ramsay was one of the original trustees). The climax of this close architectural and liturgical relationship was the Englishman George Gilbert Scott's winning the 1872 Gothic

Revival competition design for St Mary's Episcopal Cathedral, Edinburgh (built 1874–1917), which utilised a powerfully eclectic mixture of Early Gothic models.

Although *The Ecclesiologist* supported the use of Scottish architectural features as models for new Episcopal churches, historians have doubted the significance of its influence on the handful of Scottish architects who were commissioned by the Scottish Episcopal Church: the English architects they employed, on the whole, followed English fashions. Of course, an Anglican and Catholic architectural pressure group could have little impact upon a religious community dominated by the Scottish Presbyterian church, but from the late 1880s a number of ecclesiological societies were formed in Scotland. Despite this late Victorian reliance on high profile English 'Goths' for church commissions, a number of Scottish architects initially took forward Burn's innovative home-grown correct Gothic exercise, and under the influence of the broader Gothic Revival ethos – which jettisoned the concepts of proportion and symmetry, for those of rationalism and structural expression – these architects transformed the skyline facing Edinburgh's main thoroughfare. In turn, the speed of change in the fashions of revived medieval architectural styles in the mid-to-late 19th century introduced an ever-increasing diversity, which in Scotland was fuelled by Billings' source

Engraving, c.1860, showing St John's and St Cuthbert's, with the spire-like Gothic silhouette of the Sir Walter Scott Monument set between them. From J Shepherd's Beauties of Shakespeare and Burns. *SC1088523*

View, c.1890, of Edinburgh from Calton Hill (by J Patrick), showing the early 19th century St John's engulfed by trees and sandwiched between the two monumental spires of the Scott Monument and St Mary's Episcopal Cathedral. At the top left, the massive towering spire of the Victoria Hall, Castlehill, can just be seen. SC1082783

books. From the late 1830s onwards the solitary Gothic tower of St John's was joined by a flourish of important Gothic monuments, and the renowned 'Romantic Edinburgh' cityscape – with its eclectic juxtaposition of spiky Gothic spires and Classical temples – was formed. Most notable amongst the early interventions, as we saw, was the towering silhouette of Gillespie Graham's Victoria Hall, Castlehill, 1839–44 (the detailing, ironically for a Presbyterian meeting hall, provided by Pugin). The attenuated neo-Tudor Gothic entrance towers of Playfair's Free Church College, 1846–50, on the Mound, beautifully framed the Victoria Hall tower behind creating a triple-towered ensemble. But it was the tall canopied spire-like monument to Sir Walter Scott of 1840–46, by George Meikle Kemp, that created the most powerful picturesque Gothic set-piece amongst the Classical grandeur

of the New Town. The archaeological correctness initially introduced at St John's took a major leap forward when Kemp revived the detailing of the indigenous ecclesiastical Scottish Gothic of Melrose Abbey. Kemp, who worked for Burn, was a pioneer of the accurate archaeological recording of medieval monuments, and carried out extensive sketching-study tours in the 1820s and 30s. Burn's original (destroyed) open octagonal lantern design for St John's bears more than a passing resemblance to the Scott Monument's irregular and elongated profile. Could it be that the distinctive open-worked crown spire of St Giles was one of the indigenous inspirations for the lantern at St John's and in turn for the monument to Scott, which it looks towards?

This outburst of inventive secular neo-Gothic in the centre of the capital proved short-lived because, by the mid-century, the quest for a more fitting 'national' architectural style had begun to shift to the secular Scotch Baronial style. The rise of this new phase of architecture was, however, greatly influenced by Burn, in his capacity as a prolific country house designer, together with his partner (from 1841 to 1850), David Bryce.

St John's: The Halcyon Years, 1818–1899

Rev. Edward Bannerman Ramsay and the Adornment of St John's, 1827–72

Following its consecration on 19 March 1818, and first service on 20 March 1818, the pivotal and pioneering role of St John's in the wider revival of the Scottish Episcopal Church in the capital, and beyond, ensured that it would flourish. Central to this increasing momentum within the church was Rev. Edward Bannerman Ramsay (1793–1872), who was appointed curate at St John's in 1827 to assist Bishop Sandford. Following Sandford's death in 1830, Ramsay became the incumbent of St John's, and held this position until his death in 1872. Whereas Sandford had been directly involved in the resurgence of the Episcopal church in the early decades of the 19th century, Ramsay was central to the remarkable expansion of the church from the late 1830s onwards. Ramsay's most significant contribution to the wider Episcopal church was the founding of the Scottish Episcopal Church Society in 1838, to give financial aid to poor and aged clergymen and poor congregations, to assist candidates for the ministry, and to further the cause of education for that ministry. Bound up with these developments was a growing sense of missionary responsibility within the church. The society was a forerunner of the Representative Church Council, which ultimately evolved into the present-day General Synod.

1868 picturesque view of St John's south front from the graveyard of St Cuthbert's Parish Church, by G Washington Wilson. The neo-Gothic mausoleum to the Gordons of Cluny (foreground) was designed by D Bryce, and carved by P B Smith. © University of Aberdeen

Ramsay, an eloquent and popular preacher, was appointed Dean of Edinburgh in 1846. During his tenure at St John's a number of dignitaries regularly visited, including William Gladstone (who maintained strong links with Scotland and Episcopalianism). Ramsay is, however, best known for his extremely successful publication, *Reminiscences of Scottish Life and Characters*

View, c.1930, of the 1878 monument to Rev. Edward Bannerman Ramsay, designed by R Rowand Anderson, and positioned to the east of St John's. SC1088566

(twenty-two volumes published between 1858 and 1874), and following his death in 1872, Ramsay became the individual most prominently commemorated at St John's. In 1873, a statue by John Steell, under a canopy by the acclaimed Gothic Revivalist, William Burges, was initially proposed as a monument to Ramsay, but was not carried out. In 1878, a neo-Celtic twenty-six foot high granite cross, designed by Robert Rowand Anderson, was erected by public subscription on the ground east of the church – its style contrasting markedly with the English neo-Perpendicular of St John's, and symbolising Ramsay's interest in the early medieval Christian church. Within the church itself, a Moorish-inspired wall monument to Ramsay, by George Gilbert Scott (bronze, enamel and coloured stones by F A Skidmore), was erected in 1878 in the east end of the south aisle (in late 1882 it was moved to its present position on the south wall of the chancel), and a bust of Ramsay, by Steell, sits in the north-west porch.

What impact did Ramsay's growing popularity, the quickening revival of the Episcopal church as a whole, and the strengthening of St John's as an elite and wealthy congregation (in part fuelled by the influx of English families to the capital), have on the built fabric of St John's? Ramsay's greatest architectural legacy can be found in the church's interior. As outlined, the overall architectural forms of St John's, as designed and finalised by William Burn from 1815–18, remain fundamentally the same today, but the enhanced interior decoration and adornment (chiefly the windows and wall-mounted memorials), and the overall Gothic aesthetic ensemble that gives St John's its striking impact, is essentially a construct of the middle decades of the 19th century. The climax of this interior enhancement was the new projecting polygonal chancel at the east end: originally mooted in 1854, it was finally designed (1878–81), built, and lavishly adorned from 1882 onwards. Ramsay was in fact an active member of the Architectural Institute of Scotland (established in 1849 to facilitate architectural and antiquarian debate between architects, patrons and laypersons),

Painting, c.1850, of the east end, showing the shallow flat chancel simply decorated. The original east window of 1819, designed by A Geddes, was replaced in 1855–7 by Ballantine and Allan. The small gallery to the north of the chancel was installed in 1836. © St John's Episcopal Church

and gave a paper on the revived Gothic style in the session 1850–1.

Before considering the important mid-19th century installation of stained glass and memorials, the main architectural additions and alterations of Ramsay's incumbency that can be seen today, need to be briefly outlined. Because the arrival of Ramsay ushered in a period of unprecedented popularity for St John's, the demands for additional seating and in particular the extension of existing galleries and erection of new ones, became a recurring feature of St John's development. Today, the provision of galleries is exactly as it was in Burn's original design, but between 1828 and the turn of the century the provision of galleries was in a constant state of flux. The original 1815 concept for an encircling gallery had been quickly jettisoned, and only the small organ-choir gallery set in the west tower was built (for a description of the organ see below). To meet the demand for seats this small gallery was abutted in 1828 by a new larger gallery occupying the full width of the west end. In 1836, the focus for provision of new galleries moved to the east end of the church, and two new galleries were erected at either side of the altar – above the vestry and lobby beside the south-east door. In 1867 the two galleries flanking the altar were removed, and in 1912 the full-length west gallery was removed, and the balcony provision was restored to its original 1818 built form.

The reordering of St John's in the mid-19th century in accordance with liturgical developments was clearly an issue discussed by Ramsay and the Vestry. The initial 1854 plans prepared by David Bryce for a new projecting chancel came to nothing. The embellishment of the interior began in earnest in the late 1850s as the major programme of stained glass installation got underway (although new monuments were erected as early as 1830). In 1857, the baptistry, originally housed in the open south-west corner of the church, was fitted with oak paneling, and the original oak font was replaced by a marble one. The baptistry was refurbished in 1867 by Peddie & Kinnear and in 1912 a canopy of carved tiered pinnacles supported on four posts (high enough to walk underneath) was provided over the font: it was based on the font cover at St Peter Mancroft, Norwich. This font is now positioned to the south of the chancel (without canopy).

1913 view of south west corner by Bedford Lemere & Co., showing the oak pews and aisle panelling by Peddie & Kinnear of 1867, and the new font cover of 1912 housed in original baptistery to the left, by J M Dick Peddie & Forbes. The full-width gallery was also removed in 1912. SC717129

In 1865, George Gilbert Scott was approached to make changes to the internal layout and design a new chancel. Scott was paid for his plans, but the cost deterred further action. In 1867, however, a limited re-ordering and enhancement of St John's was designed by Peddie & Kinnear – an architectural firm formed in 1856 by John Dick Peddie and Charles G H Kinnear. This firm became one of Scotland's largest and most successful architectural practices of the second half of the 19th century. Kinnear (1830–94), who studied at Edinburgh University and was articled to David Bryce, was from a Fife-based land-owning family. An Episcopalian and member of St John's, he appears to have led the design work. Peddie & Kinnear removed the galleries flanking

c.1860 sketch by J T Mayne of St John's west end, showing the rebuilt late 18th century organ by George England set within the west tower. This delicate monochrome image shows the full-width gallery which was installed in 1828 (removed 1912), and the baptistry in the south-west corner (converted to the church office in 1982–3). The interior of the west end was yet to be illuminated by its colourful stained glass, and still had its box pews. © Anne Maclean of Dochgarroch

1912 design proposal for baptistry font cover by J M Dick Peddie & Forbes (for the adopted design see previous illustration). DP030516

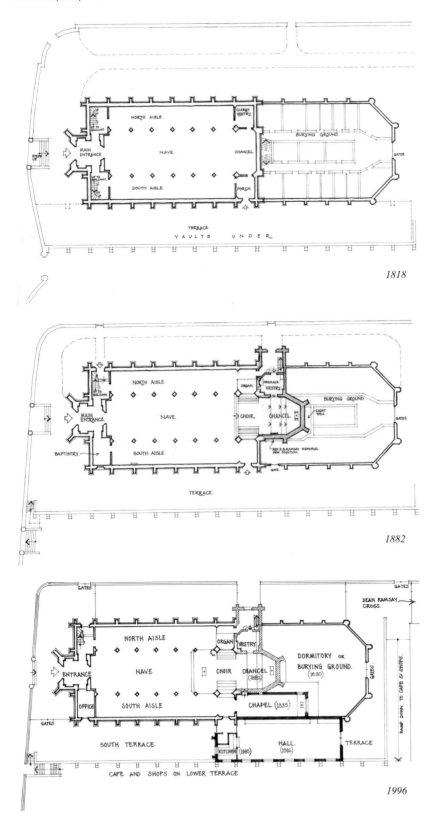

1818

1882

1996

Three ground floor plans of St John's illustrate the key developments of the church fabric from 1818–1996. Drawn by Leslie Hodgson from 1989–96. © Leslie Hodgson

the altar and formed a new exit door at the north-west of the church. The box pews were removed and replaced by heavy oak pews decorated at the ends with carvings of vine leafs, and a new pulpit and aisle panelling were installed. All were designed in a neo-Perpendicular style. The re-decoration of the interior with a stenciled colour scheme was proposed, but no evidence of this scheme having been executed has been uncovered to date. This, Peddie & Kinnear's first commission at St John's, initiated over 70 years of fruitful collaboration between the firm (and its successors), and the church: the baton of architectural responsibility appears to have passed neatly from William Burn to Peddie & Kinnear. The climax of this relationship was Peddie & Kinnear's design for the new chancel from 1872 onwards (see below).

Ramsay's other most noteworthy legacy, whilst not impacting upon the fabric of St John's itself, greatly enhanced the broader role of the church throughout the capital: this being the establishment of small churches and educational missions in growing and impoverished working-class communities outwith the elite and wealthy New Town. The social reforming agenda of Thomas Chalmers' Church of Scotland parish experiments with poor-relief in problematic working class areas clearly inspired Ramsay. In 1851, St John's decided to establish its first missionary scheme, raised funds from its congregation between 1852–3, and built a school and mission in Earl Grey Street in Edinburgh's Tollcross area. Typically, the most successful missions soon became established as independent churches and congregations. In 1863, members of the Earl Grey Street mission congregation financed and opened their own church – the Gothic Revival All Saints Episcopal Church and School, Brougham Street, designed and built by Rowand Anderson from 1866–78 (Ramsay was responsible for awarding Anderson the commission in 1864). Other linked initiatives included: a school for infants in Earl Grey Street, 1867; a mission hall of 1897 at St Peter's Place, Viewforth (later St Kentigern's, designed by John More Dick Peddie of Peddie & Kinnear); and in the 1940s, St John's briefly undertook 'missionary' work in the Niddrie peripheral housing scheme.

1965 view of high apse at All Saints' Episcopal Church, Brougham Street, Edinburgh, designed by R Rowand Anderson in 1866–78. All Saints' (later St Michael and All Saints') congregation grew from St John's first mission in the Tollcross area, and established itself as an independent church in 1863. Its dark, richly decorated altar and heavy early neo-Gothic French motifs, contrasted strongly with the delicate early-19th century aesthetic of St John's, and highlighted the ever-shifting ecclesiastical fashions of the Victorian Gothic Revival. SC1088537

Memorialising St John's: Windows and Monuments

The mid 19th century stained glass windows and numerous monuments adorning St John's merit an historical study in their own right. This present publication can only provide a limited introduction to the key works and their all-important impact on the overall visual Gothic ensemble of St John's. The windows stand as a memorial to the Forbes family and other wealthy patrons of the church, whilst the numerous wall-mounted monuments record the individual contributions made by various elite members of the congregation to the British imperial triumphs of the second half of the 19th century.

Aesthetically, the windows of St John's are important for two main reasons. From the

2005 view of lower panel memorial window to Isobel Ramsay (window 11), 1858–9, inserted as part of the first phase of stained glass windows in the aisles of St John's, by J Ballantine. SC1088544

very beginning, the new chapel was to have a prominent painted glass window in its flat-facaded east end. Designed and executed in 1817–20, it was one of the earliest examples of revived post-Reformation ecclesiastical painted glass in Scotland. The early 19th century revival of stained glass initially evolved in the domestic rather than ecclesiastical field – with indigenous craftsmen practicing in Scotland from the 1830s onwards. Secondly, in 1855, St John's employed the stained glass painter James Ballantine (1808–77) to replace the deteriorated 1817 window, and to design stained glass throughout the church. By the mid-1840s, as we will see below, Ballantine had become an established authority, and leader, in the growing field of Scottish stained glass production. His highly-successful firm developed into a burgeoning dynastic studio which dominated ecclesiastical projects in Edinburgh in the mid-late 19th century. Between 1855 and 1935 the firm was employed to furnish St John's with stained glass.

The St John's windows fall broadly into five chronological categories: the original designs for the 1817–20 east window (replaced in 1855 and incorporated into the new chancel in 1882); the main nave windows of 1857–61; the second and third completion phase of nave windows of 1874 and 1930; the new chancel windows of 1882–6; and the new chapel windows of 1935.

The original window of the flat east end, although now completely replaced, highlighted the important role the Episcopal church played in the revival of stained glass windows in early 19th century Scotland. The post-Reformation church had denounced artistic adornment – including decorative stained glass – which resulted in the destruction of essentially all windows. It was the non-established Episcopal church that pioneered its reintroduction into ecclesiastical buildings in the early 19th century.

The Original East Window

Forbes took full responsibility for the provision of the east end window (a six-light window surmounted by a wheel window of radiating tracery), and money was raised from the congregation. Initial attempts to obtain medieval coloured glass from redundant English windows (via an agent in Norwich) were abandoned, and Forbes employed the portrait painter George Sanders in early 1817. He produced a design comprising rows of saints, and rows of coats of arms in the lower compartments. William Raphael Eginton of Birmingham was employed to execute the window. Not only were there almost no remaining examples of stained glass left in post-Reformation Scotland for indigenous artists to draw upon, the skills and techniques had almost disappeared. The earliest known 19th century

Calotype, c.1845, titled Edinburgh Ale (by D O Hill and R Adamson), showing Ballantine (left), drinking with George Bell and David Octavious Hill in the latter's home. © Scottish National Portrait Gallery

commissions for painted glass in Scotland were therefore by Eginton's firm, and St John's was his first notable ecclesiastical design. A month before the chapel opened in March 1818, Eginton expressed unhappiness about Sanders' design and suggested the figures of saints should either be beneath a canopy or on small pedestals with coats of arms at the sides. By the opening, the window remained unfinished. Eventually, the 14th century Gothic formula of coats of arms of local benefactors set below figures was adopted, and in July 1818, following disputes over cost with Eginton, Forbes was forced to turn to the artist Andrew Geddes to improve the composition of the overall design by taking out canopies and removing shields in the bottom panels. By May 1819, Geddes had prepared drawings for twelve apostles standing on pedestals: Eginton then took down the already-erected windows and inserted the apostles.

By the mid-1850s the original painted east window had deteriorated seriously. Between 1855 and 1857 a replacement window designed

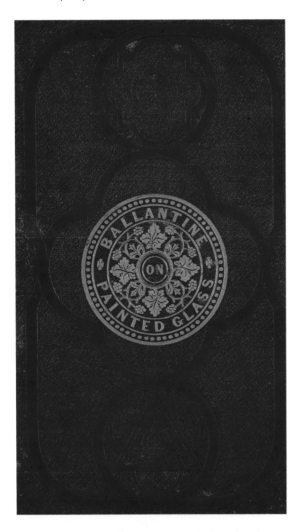

Embossed front cover and sample page, above, from J Ballantine's A Treatise on Painted Glass, *published 1845. DP033148 & DP003149*

by Ballantine and Allan was commissioned and installed: the twelve radiating sections of the wheel compartments now had angels playing musical instruments. And the twelve new apostles were seated on clouds, with their emblems in the two sections of the six-lights below. These apostles were apparently adapted from designs by Friedrich Overback. In 1882, this replacement east window was removed and incorporated in the new chancel (for the description of the existing chancel windows, see below).

James Ballantine, whose firm dominated the stained glass work at St John's, was born in West Port, Edinburgh, the son of a brewer. According to various accounts, Ballantine was apprenticed to the acclaimed topographical artist David Roberts and the house painter Archibald Cleland. It was as a house painter that he took classes in 1827 at the Trustees Academy in Edinburgh, and studied anatomy at Edinburgh University to improve his draughtsmanship. In 1828 he founded his own glass painting and house decorating business, Ballantine and Allan, in a short-lived partnership with George Allan. In 1845 he published *A Treatise on Painted Glass*, the first Scottish book on stained glass in the modern period. He was highly critical of the indiscriminate copying of medieval glass. Ballantine was the chief 'revivalist' of stained glass in Scotland – a movement that burgeoned in Scotland under the influence of Pugin and the Tractarian movement. Whilst other craftsmen and artists worked in this field, it was the gifted businessman Ballantine who exploited the market with vigour. Ballantine was also a poet and writer, a recognised authority on Robert Burns, and counted amongst his friends prominent cultural figures such as the artists David Roberts and Horatio McCulloch, and the pioneering photographer David Octavius Hill.

The foundations of Ballantine's highly successful dynastic firm were established when his sample panel won the 1843 national competition for the stained glass in London's House of Lords, despite his being relatively unknown at that time. In Scotland, his earliest known surviving commission was the stained glass for W H Playfair's Donaldson's School Chapel, Edinburgh, from 1841, and in 1846 he installed the stained glass at the private Chapel of St Anthony the Eremite, Murthly, Perthshire. The extension of the latter historic chapel was designed by Gillespie Graham (1845–6) – possibly with assistance from Pugin. Ballantine's most significant early secular commission came in 1847 for the four armorial panels of the prestigious Walter Scott Monument (cartoon by David Roberts). Unlike most other commercial 19th century studios, Ballantine's was almost exclusively an ecclesiastical firm. Running parallel with his scheme for St John's, he obtained the first stained glass commission for the Church of Scotland proper (rather than private chapels), with the restoration of Old Greyfriars, Edinburgh, in 1856, and with this project Ballantine broke the post-Reformation resistance to stained glass. The firm's most prestigious project was the series of windows for St Giles', Edinburgh (with artist Robert Herdman of the noted Gothic Revival ecclesiastical manufacturing family), of 1872–1905. Ballantine died in 1877 and was succeeded by his son Alexander (1840–1906), who established the partnership Ballantine & Gardiner from 1892–1905, and was in turn succeeded by his son James Ballantine II (1878–1940).

The Aisle Windows, 1857–1930

From 1818 until 1857 all the windows, except the east window, were of clear glass. By 1861 all the aisle windows (except two to the west) were filled. The studio of Ballantine was responsible for all of the windows in the aisle windows, with work being carried out in three stages – all still remaining today. The first and largest phase, 1857–61, consisted of ten out of the twelve aisle windows (the aisle windows are numbered 1–12 clockwise from the westernmost end of the north aisle, and details on a hand-written plaque are placed beneath each window). The windows were divided vertically into three lights by mullions, and below were three lower panels. In the top dominant panels, the windows illustrate the life and deeds of Christ (well suited to Ballantine's figurative work),

and the lower panels contain heraldic shields and form memorials to the Forbes family, other notable trustees, key clergy, and accomplished members of the congregation. The stylistic harmony of the brightly-coloured mosaic glass was created with the dominant use of alternating reds and blues (Christ is clothed in red), and the architectural forms of Gothic pinnacles and crockets. Slightly thicker glass was used in parts to give a darker hue, and a thin line of clear glass is placed next to the stone surround so that the coloured glass does not appear diffused against the dark surround.

2005 view of memorial window to James and Ann Strange (window 6), 1857, one of the first two stained glass aisle windows designed by J Ballantine. SC1088546

The first two easternmost aisle windows were erected in 1857 as memorials to James Stuart Strange, a wealthy businessman who had made his fortune investing in the East India Company and other ventures in the British Empire (window 6), and the Paterson family (window 7). Other notable memorial windows followed: in 1858–9 two windows were erected as a memorial to Isobella Ramsay (wife of Rev. Edward Bannerman Ramsay, died 1858, window 11), and to George Forbes (banker, vestryman of St John's, and brother of William Forbes, died 1857, window 8); in 1859–60, windows to Sir William Forbes, St John's original leading benefactor (window 4), and

2007 detail view of memorial window to James Clerk Rattray and William Hay Newton (window 10), 1861, by J Ballantine. The upper panels of the first phase aisle windows illustrated the life and deeds of Christ: this detail depicts the building of the temple. DP020736

2005 view of memorial window to George Sholto Douglas, Earl of Morton (window 5), 1860, inserted nearing the end of the first phase of stained glass aisle windows, by J Ballantine. SC1088554

his brother-in-law and second of the three most important trustees, Colin Mackenzie of Portmore (died 1830, window 3) were inserted; in July 1860 windows were erected to William's son, the banker Charles Hay Forbes (died 1859, window 2), and George Swinton, Secretary to the Governor General of India (died 1854, window 9); and finally in 1861 a window to the third trustee, James Clerk Rattray, judge in the Exchequer Court (died 1831, window 10), was installed. Coats of arms of all those commemorated were in the lower panels.

The first-phase windows on the north aisle depict the following scenes: the Good Samaritan and Jesus walking on water (window 6); the Garden of Gethsemane, Jesus blessing the bread, and the man of sorrows (window 5); Mary anointing Jesus' feet, teaching humility, and Jesus with Nicodemus (window 4); raising of Jairus' daughter or of Lazarus, giving sight to the blind, and the marriage at Cana (window 3); 'Follow Christ', 'Suffer the Little Children', and St Peter at the gates of heaven (window 2). The south aisle windows depict the following scenes: visiting the stranger, feeding the hungry and visiting the sick (window 7); feeding the thirsty, clothing the naked, and visiting the prisoner (window 8); the resurrection (window 9); building the temple (window 10); and Mary and Martha (window 11).

The completion of the aisle windows in phase two (i.e., the two westernmost windows of the north and south aisles) was carried out by Ballantine's son Alexander in 1874. These differed stylistically

2007 detail view of memorial window to Isobella Ramsay (window 11), 1858–9, by J Ballantine. This scene depicts Jesus in the house of Mary and Martha. DP020740

from Ballantine's first windows, and comprised smaller pieces of glass with formal geometrical floral patterns (inspired by the Arts and Crafts Movement), and used less vivid colours. The south window (number 12) was inserted as a memorial to Bannerman Ramsay, and depicted Jesus in the temple, as the good shepherd, and catching an excess of fish. The north window was a memorial to James Moncrieff Melville and depicted Jesus as ruler and judge of the world flanked by angels (number 1). The completion of the aisle windows in 1930 by James Ballantine II, consisted of two windows inserted as memorials: the lower part of window 12 to Mrs Wade illustrated the baptism of Christ by John the Baptist (with his attribute the eagle); and the other, to James Lutyens Mansfield, depicted the transfiguration.

Memorials, from 1831

St John's has a unique collection of mid-19th century neo-Gothic and neo-Tudor marble wall-monuments adorning the aisle walls. Set between the brightly-coloured windows with their Gothic detailing, the disciplined tablets commemorate (with some exceptions) members of the congregation who died in British 19th century imperial wars, and greatly enhance the overall neo-Gothic aesthetic of the interior. The distinctiveness of the St John's war memorials lies in the fact that so many commemorate high-ranking individuals, in contrast to group regimental memorials such as those adorning St Giles' Cathedral's west end. The tradition of commemorating individual soldiers of high social status, common after the Napoleonic wars, was long continued at St John's. These individual privately-funded memorials are not war memorials in the collective 20th century sense, and the numerous smaller memorials of World War I and II in St John's are similarly to individuals.

The series of neo-Gothic tablets mainly commemorated men who were killed in action, or as a result of it, but the first wall monuments were to prominent clergymen. In 1830–1, a large marble monument to St John's founder, Bishop Sandford, was erected (now in the church offices – former baptistery – at the west end). In 1842, two further monuments were erected facing each other in the easternmost ends of the north and south aisles: the most notable being that to Rev.

2007 view of neo-Gothic memorial tablet to Rev. James Walker, Bishop of Edinburgh, 1842, by Wallace and Whyte. DP020724

James Walker, Bishop of Edinburgh (following Sandford) from 1830 until his death in 1841. All three monuments were by the sculptors Wallace and Whyte. A number of memorials to key members of the congregation followed. In the south aisle are a memorial to Captain William Hunter, who actually died in church in April 1843, and one to Lady Elizabeth Bannerman Ramsay, who died in 1844. The provenance and authorship of the wall monument to Mary Arbuthnot, wife of a former Lord Provost and original trustee of St John's, is not clear. The tablet of 1822–3, attributed to the great 19th century sculptor John Flaxman, depicted two mourning figures (faith and charity) in classical dress, but was not recorded in St John's church records until 1873. It may have been moved to its present position on the easternmost section of the south aisle above the door to the church hall

from elsewhere. Also of note are the later heraldic shields set below the clearstory windows which display, to the north, the coats of arms of previous rectors of St John's, and to the south, coats of arms of various bishops of Edinburgh.

The memorials to military men from 1841 onwards testify to the genteel imperialism of the original worshippers of St John's: represented are the Indian, Afghan, Crimean and South African wars which characterized British imperialist expansion in the latter half of the 19th century. The bulk of the military monuments are mounted on the north aisle and at the west end of the church, but the earliest, on the south aisle, was to Captain John Woodburn of the 44th Bengal Native Infantry, who died in 1841 in the first British Afghan intervention of 1838–42: from the early 19th century Afghanistan was an uneasy neutral zone between the Russian and the British Indian empires, around which 'the Great Game' was played. The complex mid-19th century relationship between the activities of the economic empire of the British East Indian Company until the 'Indian Mutiny' of 1857, and the native population, is illustrated in the individual monuments at St John's. In the north aisle are memorials to Lieutenant Douglas Charles Turing Beatson of the 14th Bengal Native Infantry, who died at Sobraon in 1846, aged 24, and Captain James Robertson of the 9th regiment of the Madras Native Infantry, and Assistant Commissioner General, who died in passage in 1851. High-ranking quasi-civil servants for the East India Company in Bengal, such as Alex Breuere Tod, who died in 1853, are also commemorated. Two deceased soldiers, who perhaps died as a result of the 1857 uprising, are commemorated in two monuments placed in the west end: Captain Alexander Laurence Tweedie, of the 36th Royal Madras, who died in passage from India in 1858; and Lieutenant James Cruickshank of the 36th Madras Native Infantry, who died at sea in 1857. Individual casualties of the Crimean War of 1853–6 (a British and French attempt to halt Russian expansion), are represented in the series of marble monuments. In the north aisle stand memorials to Captain Edward Stanley of Her Majesty's 57th Regiment, who died in the Crimea at the battle of Inkerman in 1854 whilst in command of his regiment at Cathcart Hill, and Major-General Sir John Campbell, who served in the first

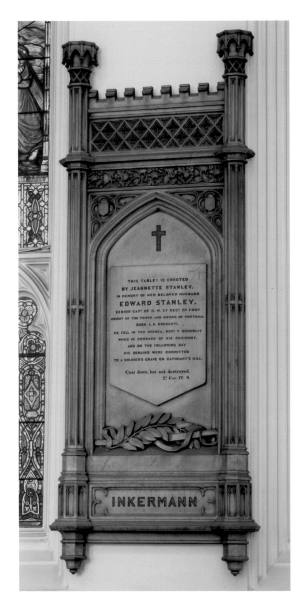

2007 view of neo-Gothic memorial tablet to Captain Edward Stanley, who died in the Crimea at the battle of Inkerman in 1854. DP020718

Burmese War, and commanded the 38th regiment at the battles of Alma and Inkerman. Both men were buried on 'Cathcart Hill', near Sebastopol. In the west end is a memorial to Lieutenant-Colonel Thomas Graham of the Royal Regiment, who died on his return from the Crimea in November 1855. Also on the north aisle is the curious brass plaque memorial to John S S Forbes of the United States Cavalry, who was killed at the battle of Little Big Horn (Custer's last stand) in 1876.

The New Chancel, from 1878–89

As outlined, the Gothic Revival polemics of Pugin, the Tractarian movement, and the later Ecclesiological Society, had a strong impact on the architecture and art of the Scottish Episcopal Church from the 1840s onwards. In terms of church design, the Gothic Revival promoted the adoption of medieval-inspired church plans, with a deep chancel, and a reliance on the decorative arts. Under Ramsay's direction, St John's sought to conform to these new fashionable principles. The abandonment of Burn's flat east end, and extension of the church to the east, was at the forefront of church fabric concerns despite finance being limited. George Gilbert Scott's unexecuted plans of 1865 included a new chancel, but then in May 1872 he was again paid to prepare plans for a new chancel. Ramsay died in 1872, and the scheme was not built for reasons of cost. Gilbert Scott's attention was clearly drawn towards the more financially lucrative architectural competition to build a new Episcopal cathedral in Edinburgh in 1872, which he won. Gilbert Scott, knighted in 1872, was Britain's most prolific Gothic Revival architect. His practice secured thirteen commissions from the Scottish Episcopal Church, and his main ecclesiastical patron and admirer in mid-19th century Scotland was Alexander Penrose Forbes, Bishop of Brechin (nephew of Sir William Forbes, St John's original lead trustee).

Perspective drawing of Peddie & Kinnear's first design of 1879 for the new chancel, illustrated in Rev. G F Terry's Memorials of the Church of St John the Evangelist, 1911. Its attribution in Memorials *to J M Dick Peddie – John Peddie's son who joined his father in partnership in 1879 – and date of 1854 is puzzling, but it was most probably a sketch after the 1879 design. © St John's Episcopal Church*

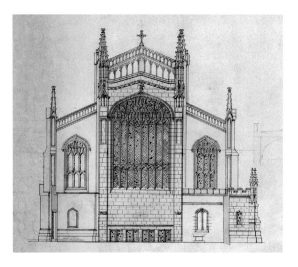

1879 east elevation of the first worked-up design for the new chancel and vestry by Peddie & Kinnear, showing the flat-ended proposal. SC836033

The year 1872 marked a turning point in the power politics of the Scottish Episcopal Church in Edinburgh and beyond. The new chapel of St John's had been a pioneer, both in architectural and religious terms, in the early 19th century revival of the church, and it continued to play a central role during the period of Ramsay's incumbency. By the 1870s, following Ramsay's death, and ironically

1881 east and north elevations of the final design for the new chancel and vestry by Peddie & Kinnear, showing the polygonal-ended apse. SC836049

as a direct result of his laying the foundations of a financially stronger national church, the momentum for new church building was reaching its peak. Building on the grand Gothic Revival city church-building programme, initiated in the late-1840s with William Butterfield's St Ninian's Episcopal Cathedral, Perth (1849), and St Paul's Episcopal Cathedral, Dundee, by Gilbert Scott (1853–5), new larger projects followed. In the late 1860s, Inverness Episcopal Cathedral was designed and built by Alexander Ross (1866–9), and the grand St Mary's Episcopal Church, Glasgow, by Gilbert Scott in 1871–8 (later raised to cathedral status in 1907), was also embarked upon. With the establishment of a trust in 1870 to build the massive and high-profile St Mary's Episcopal Cathedral in Edinburgh, the religious and symbolic power of the church in the capital drifted away from the smaller churches like St John's and St Paul's, York Place (the latter had in fact contained the Bishop's chair following Sandford's death, and it passed to the new St Mary's Cathedral thereafter). The new cathedral subsequently became the focus for national unity of the church.

But by 1878, Kinnear was preparing plans for a new chancel. Gilbert Scott died in early 1879, and the passing of the job to Kinnear was perhaps made easier. The first worked-up proposal of 1879 consisted of a square-ended projecting bay with a large single east-end window – very

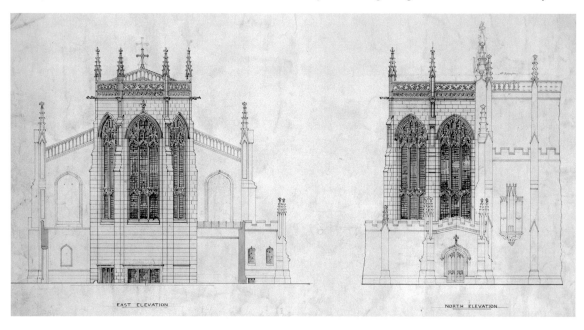

EAST ELEVATION

NORTH ELEVATION

View, c.1910, showing the east end with its extended chancel. SC1077294

much in keeping with the flat-ended collegiate neo-Perpendicular models originally adopted by Burn – set within the original burial enclosure. Despite being approved by the Vestry, Kinnear was forced to produce a second design in late 1881 because full permission to build upon existing burial plots was not obtained. George Bruce, W.S. (whose grandfather had purchased a family plot in the west

end of the enclosure in 1823), successfully halted the encroachment upon his family burial ground by the new chancel. As a result, the chancel had to be modified by having its corners cut-off at an angle. The new chancel consisted of one aisle-less bay and a new three-sided polygonal apse: the existing aisle, which housed the previous chancel, now accommodated the choir (a porch and vestry on the north side, and a new hall under the chancel, were also built). The adoption of a polygonal apse was clearly a major design shift, but interestingly its use harked back to clear Scottish Gothic precedents,

One of several undated sketch designs for a new stone reredos by Peddie & Kinnear. This sketch probably dates for the late 1880s, and is the closest in form to that finally built in 1889. DP030518

View, c.1911, of the chancel nearing the completion of its interior adornment from 1881–1913, and just before the erection of the rood screen. The stone neo-Gothic triptych reredos (a memorial to Admiral Sir William Edmonstone) is set below the three new stained glass memorial windows. The choir canopied stalls and panelling, based on the late-Gothic choir stalls at King's College Chapel, Aberdeen, were designed by Peddie & Forbes. SC466205

rather than the adopted English neo-Perpendicular sources, such as the 1504 apse at Holy Rood, Stirling, and the 15th century apse at St Michael's, Linlithgow. In November 1881, Kinnear's new design was finally accepted at an estimated cost of £3,217 – which did not include the cost of reredos or stained glass, which were paid for by private donations. On 2 December 1882, Henry Cotterill, Bishop of Edinburgh, consecrated the completed chancel.

St John's employed two London studios to design and insert the three stained glass end windows of the new chancel. In 1882, the centre east window was filled with stained glass as a memorial to John Blackwood (died 1879), publisher, and his son John Alex (died 1882), by Clayton & Bell. The south window (to the right), also by Clayton & Bell, was a dual memorial to William Huett (lower, died 1882) and Edward James Jackson (top). In 1886–7, Heaton, Butler & Bayne filled the north chancel window (to the left) as a memorial to Eliza Jackson (died 1885). All three windows, in a neo-15th century Gothic style, depicted scenes of the life of Christ. In 1882, as part of the chancel's stained glass programme, the 1855–7 Ballantine glass of the flat east end (depicting the twelve apostles) was inserted in the north and south walls of the pre-existing aisle incorporated in the chancel.

Further adornment of the chancel continued. Between 1869–70, Peddie & Kinnear had prepared several sketch designs for a new reredos (a decorated screen, set behind the altar to enhance its visual importance), but it was not until 1889 that a new reredos was placed at the back of the chancel below the central window. On 17 February 1889, it was dedicated as a memorial to Admiral Sir William Edmonstone of Duntreath, 4th Baronet, a distinguished naval commander, who died in February 1888. Peddie & Kinnear provided a Caen stone neo-Gothic triptych of 15th century style, executed by James Kerr. The three carved pointed arches each contained panels of painted tiles and gold mosaic (by W B Simpson & Son, London): in the central arch, is a figure of Christ with pastoral staff and holding a Eucharistic cup; to the left, the Virgin Mary (holding her emblem of a lily and a closed book); and to the right, St John the Evangelist (holding his gospel with his emblematic figure of an eagle at his feet).

St John's maintained a strong musical tradition throughout the 19th century, and the status and condition of the organ was a constant concern. The first organ (built in the late 18th century by George England), was installed in 1818 high in the original organ-choir gallery set in the west tower, and was re-built in 1835 and 1853. In 1880, it was moved to the north of the developing new chancel. The second existing organ was installed on the same site in 1901–2 by the accomplished English organ-builder Henry Willis, of Willis and Sons, who attempted to use as much of the original George England pipework as possible. It was rebuilt by Rushworth and Dreaper in 1930, and modified by R C Goldsmith in 1973–4. In 2003–4, repair and restoration of the organ was carried out by Geoffrey Coffin, who aimed to return the instrument to a condition not dissimilar to that built by Henry Willis in 1901–2.

2005 interior view of chancel today, showing the restored (1982–3) painted panels of the reredos. Beyond the stalls on the right, is the Moorish-inspired wall monument to Rev. Edward Bannerman Ramsay by G Gilbert Scott, 1878. It was moved to its present position in 1882. SC1088558

Expansion and Conservation

1900 to the Present Day

St John's was a pioneer, in architectural and religious terms, in the early-19th century revival of the Scottish Episcopal Church. Throughout the remainder of the 19th century, St John's witnessed growing popularity, expansion, and a new focus on 'home' missionary activities. The remarkable revival of the nationwide Episcopal church, from the 1830s onwards, and its associated church-building drive, culminated in the late 19th century programme of large city churches and cathedrals throughout Scotland, and by the close of the century the nationwide church had nearly 300 congregations and 116,000 members. By the 1880s, as the Episcopal Church expanded, St John's ultimately lost its pivotal role, but it in turn benefited from the wider continued growth in the early decades of the 20th century. By 1921, the nationwide Scottish Episcopal Church had 147,000 members. St John's remained an active, outward-looking and wealthy city-centre church, with an established pedigree. By the early 1960s, it had a large congregation of 700, even as the national Episcopal Church had begun to suffer a decline from the 1950s onwards. By the close of the 20th century, St John's was recognised as one of the key historic buildings within a newly designated World Heritage Site, had undergone a careful multi-million state-assisted restoration programme, and had diversified by opening the Cornerstone Coffee House in 1971, the Cornerstone Bookshop in 1985, and the Peace and Justice Centre in 1986.

1902 view of St John's from the west, before the road widening of 1930 and the creation of the vaults under the Lothian Road pavement. © Yerbury Photography, SC1077303

1913 interior view of nave and chancel by Bedford Lemere & Co., showing the newly-completed rood screen and cross (in 1974 the screen was removed, but the suspended cross still remains). The new and re-positioned organ, of 1901–2, can also be seen to the left of the chancel. SC717125

1911 visit of King George V and Queen Mary, showing the stands erected at St John's to view the state entry through Edinburgh's west end. SC1088539

The architectural expansion and adornment of St John's, by the architectural successors of the Peddie & Kinnear practice, continued apace in the early decades of the 20th century. The four key projects in this period were: the 1912–13 programme of works by J M Dick Peddie & Forbes (John More Dick Peddie, John Peddie's son, joined his father in partnership in 1879); the new large vestry hall to the south-east of 1914–16 (also by Peddie & Forbes); the new Morning Chapel of 1934–5 by W J Walker Todd (who had taken over practice in 1921, following J M Dick Peddie's death – the latter is commemorated in a plaque at the west end of the church); and in 1937, the creation of five new rooms excavated out of the existing space below the nave of the church.

In 1909, Rev. George Frederick Terry, the author of *Memorials of the Church of St John the Evangelist* (1911), became the rector at St John's, and held the post until his death in 1919. Prior to his ordination he was an architect, and he immediately established a fund for the cleaning, painting and restoration of the church, including stone repair and re-pointing. An inscribed panel (set within a niche below the organ to the north of the chancel) commemorated Terry's commitment to the fabric of St John's, who 'laboured unsparingly to promote the beauty of this church'. Fundraising appears to have been one of Terry's strengths: for the 1911 visit of King George V and Queen Mary, a state entry through Edinburgh's west end, which passed by St John's, the opportunity to raise money was avidly exploited. Stands were erected between the church and railings, seats were sold, and a profit of £516 was made. Spectators watched as the dignitaries

entered Princes Street through a triumphal arch bedecked with banners, flowers and flags of St Andrew and St George. For the July 1937 state visit of King George VI and Queen Elizabeth stands were similarly erected and the money raised (£300) was given to Edinburgh Royal Infirmary. It was under Terry's direction that the enhancement of the chancel was continued by Peddie & Forbes. The choir stalls and carved oak panelling of the chancel were carved in 1910, based on the rare surviving late-Gothic choir stalls at King's College Chapel, Aberdeen, of 1520. This choice of Aberdeen as an architectural source by the architect illustrated the influence of the newly-formed Scottish Ecclesiological Society, who demanded that church adornment and design should employ archaeologically correct and indigenous Scottish Gothic revivalism. Ironically, the influence of the Tractarian movement in the art and architecture of

2007 view of Morning Chapel by W J Walker Todd, 1934–5, with its squat gate screen closed (by Ian G Lindsay, 1936–7). DP032673

the Scottish Episcopal Church in the late 19th and early 20th centuries greatly stimulated the renewal of the indigenous Scottish traditions of the church. The commonly held view amongst the Presbyterian church-goers, and the wider general public, that the Episcopal Church was fundamentally 'English', was continually challenged, and in 1929 the *Scottish Book of Common Prayer* finally replaced the English one.

In 1912, an East Anglian-type rood screen (with cross above) was erected between the chancel and the nave. Of carved oak (by John S Gibson), it had seven bays with the two end bays canted backwards to the choir. The lower parts of each bay consisted of solid carved linen fold-type panels, the middle section was open, and the top section had rich carved open tracery, topped by a bold cornice of enriched carving and trelliswork, which supported six upright angels. Above the screen, suspended from the ceiling by three decorated iron rods, was the large rood cross with carved floriated arms. In 1974, the rood screen was removed (but the suspended cross still remains), and part of it was re-erected in the south east chapel of St Mary's Episcopal Cathedral, Edinburgh. In 1931, a new gilded wrought iron hexagonal sanctuary lamp for the chancel was gifted by Miss H Fraser. The large beautifully detailed lamp was designed by the artist David Young Cameron (1865–1945), and made by Haddon Brothers, Roseburn, Edinburgh.

The third significant 20th century addition to St John's was a large vestry hall abutting the south wall of the east burial ground at the east end of the terrace, built in the early war years of 1914–16. Objections from Edinburgh Corporation were overcome and the much-needed hall was inconspicuously tucked behind the south east end of the church. Following Rev. George Frederick Terry's death in 1919, his family wanted to erect a chapel in his memory, but the approved scheme was abandoned because permission from the owner of one of the burial plots effected by the extension was not obtained. The families' wish, however, finally came to fruition in the mid 1930s. The small rectangular Morning Chapel, designed by W J Walker Todd, 1934–5, was built between the south wall of the chancel and the north wall of the hall. In 1933, prior to work beginning, efforts were made to trace the descendents or heirs of families over whose burial plots the chapel was to be built. Of

Front cover of St John's Magazine, October 1929. © St John's Episcopal Church

the three family burial grounds, only one, Skene of Rubislaw (for James Skene, see above), was traced: three bronze plaques listing the members of the families were placed on the south wall, and the chapel was consecrated on 18 April 1935. Todd designed a low cambered roof of Scots oak, with a carved cornice encrusted with angels (carved by Scott Morton and Andrew Lunn). The chapel window, by James Ballantine II, depicted Jesus praying by the Sea of Galilee, and was a memorial to Terry. In 1935, Ian G Lindsay (then a young conservation-orientated architect in the practice of Orphoot, Whiting & Lindsay) designed a communion rail, cross and candlesticks for the chapel, as a memorial to his parents. Lindsay had also originally produced a simple single-bay design for the south chapel as a memorial to his father in 1933 (George Herbert Lindsay, vestryman at St John's, died in 1932 and is commemorated on the

1913 interior view, by Bedford Lemere & Co., of chancel rood screen (removed 1974). SC717127

Sketch, c.1961, by J Brian Crossland in 'Church of St John the Evangelist', Scotsman, 24 June, 1961 – one of a series of articles on key Edinburgh churches. © Scotsman Publications

council, to allow the vaults under the south terrace and under Lothian Road pavement to be converted to public air-raid shelters. On completion the shelters accommodated over 850 people.

In the early postwar period the fabric of St John's changed little, and the focus of activity now shifted to ad hoc maintenance and repair (a fabric fund was started in 1928). Alterations made before the mid-1970s were subject to fluctuating liturgical fashions and the views of individual incumbents at St John's. In 1949, the 1889 reredos – now considered 'unworthy' and distracting to the eye – had heavy curtains hung over it. During his rectorship, Rev. G F Terry had continually altered the reredos, which he believed to be 'cold and forbidding' and out of keeping with the neo-Perpendicular forms of St John's. In his defence, he cited experts, such as the celebrated architect Sir Robert Lorimer (an Episcopalian), who apparently said that it 'spoiled' St John's chancel. In 1918, Terry added stone cresting to the top of the reredos, and gold leaf to the whole of the carved work. In 1974, the handsome 1912 rood screen was also removed. The government department responsible for historic building control was the Historic Buildings Branch of Scottish Development (predecessors of what is now Historic Scotland). It had existed since 1946, but for several reasons its statutory effectiveness was limited until the early 1970s, and, moreover churches in use (such as St John's) were in fact exempt from controls if internal alterations to the church fabric were made.

communion rail), but Walker Todd's more ambitious chapel was built. In 1936–7, Lindsay designed a beautiful squat gate screen to the chapel as a memorial to Margaret Isabella Inglis and Harriet Christiana Fraser.

In 1937, under Rev. Charles Henry Richie's rectorship, the space below the nave and south aisle of the church was excavated and converted into five new rooms to accommodate the booming community activities of the church. The fund-raising scheme for these works culminated in the 'Catacombs Fair' in May 1937 in the Assembly Rooms, Edinburgh. During World War II the rooms were used as rest rooms for service personnel, and between 1940 and 1942 over 6,000 service personnel slept there, and were cared for by members of the congregation. St John's had also agreed in late 1939, at the request of the city

1982 view of St John's congregation. © St John's Episcopal Church

May 1988 view of mounted painted mural (titled 'Remember the Dead of Kassinga') by the Artists for Justice and Peace, clipped onto the exterior of St John's east dormitory wall. The blackened appearance of the stone walls of St John's was transformed the following year, when approval was finally given by Historic Scotland for its stone cleaning in 1989. SC1104859

But by the 1980s, as the architectural conservation lobby gained momentum, increased government financial support became available for restoration projects, and St John's became the beneficiary of a number of high-profile grant schemes. Indeed, the early 1980s proved to be a turning point for the historic fabric of St John's. From 1981, a specialist architectural conservation practice, T M Gray & Associates (renamed Gray, Marshall & Associates in 1985), became architects to St John's and began a long association with the church; and in 1982, Rev. Neville Chamberlain, Canon of Lincoln Cathedral, was appointed rector. Under his dynamic direction, between 1982–3 the chancel was re-ordered and extended to accommodate a new oak communion table (by craftsman Christopher Holmes), and the baptistery was converted into a new church office. The reredos, which had been covered by a fabric curtain since 1949, was revealed, and the painted panels were restored by the painting conservator Rab Snowden. Running parallel to this initial fabric restoration, under Chamberlain's leadership, St John's diversified and grew.

In 1985, the space occupied by the Cornerstone Coffee House on the lower terrace (opened in 1971 for use as an ecumenical outreach project

in conjunction with the Council of West End Churches) was extended to form the new Cornerstone Bookshop. The bookshop and the new Peace and Justice Centre were officially opened in July 1986 by David Steel MP, then leader of the Liberal Party. Chamberlain was also responsible for initiating the often-controversial series of mounted painted murals, clipped to the exterior of the dormitory walls facing Princes Street as part of the Peace Festival in August 1982. The mural displays became a regular feature at St John's, and since 1982, 150 have been created by artists such as Mike Greenlaw, Paul Grime and Joyce Changes, covering subjects from the 'troubles' in Northern Ireland to the detention of prisoners at Guantanamo Bay, Cuba. Chamberlain later recalled in 2007 (which marked the 25th anniversary of the mural scheme), how the project aimed to 'reach out, engage, and communicate a contemporary gospel, with the thousands of people who flooded past the church daily'.

2005 view of nave, showing extended chancel platform. SC1088557

2005 interior view of north aisle, nave and chancel. SC1088556

The restoration of the stained glass windows, the controversial issue of stone repairs and cleaning, and the overall long-term condition of St John's, became the key church-fabric concerns of the congregation in the mid-1980s (although the fabric condition was a central concern for the congregation, the shifting patterns of worship and service to the community fundamentally drove change). Stone cleaning had been first mooted by the church in 1959, and discussions were held in 1961 with the Ministry of Works. The experts presciently discouraged cleaning, arguing that it would be harmful to the stone. In 1984, the Vestry commissioned a broad-ranging condition report for St John's, and between 1985 and 1993, an ambitious 10-year restoration scheme was begun by Gray, Marshall & Associates (led by Tom Gray and Jocelyn Cunliffe). A major public funding package was sought to boost church funds, and was secured from Historic Scotland (in the form of a Historic Buildings Council Grant), Lothian and Edinburgh Enterprise, and Edinburgh District

Council. The church launched the *Church of St John the Evangelist Appeal* to raise £200,000 for the first phase of restoration works. A report on the bulging stained glass windows of the aisles, by Patrick Ross-Smith, highlighted their extremely poor condition, and in 1985–88, each window panel was recorded, removed, and transported to the Salisbury Cathedral Works Organisation to be cleaned, repaired (replaced if required), and returned to Edinburgh. In 1987, negotiations over the provision of grants to allow stone cleaning began, trials were carried out in 1988, and agreement was reached in 1989 to use a poultice method (ProSoco T-1217), which was applied in sections and removed after twenty-four hours. Four contractors carried out the work, and it was carefully monitored by Robert Gordon's Institute of Technology. Chemical cleaning of stone was then considered less harmful (although it left deposits of salt on the surface), but even when great care was taken, such as at St John's, heritage experts were 'horrified' to see salt coming out of the stone after the poultices were removed. A parallel programme of stone repair, roof repair, new floodlighting, landscaping, and restoration of the railings, was carried out. Also as a condition of state funding, the popular three-to-four panel mural paintings on the dormitory walls, had to be reduced to one removable panel hung between two poles. At an event to mark the completion of the restoration project in 1993, David Walker, Chief Inspector of Historic Buildings at Historic Scotland admitted the authorities had been 'a bit difficult about the stone cleaning', and that the retention of an 'uninterrupted view' of St John's was foremost in their minds.

In 2001, Benjamin Tindall Architects became the church architects for St John's. An internal re-lighting scheme which included the installation of a new modern chandelier, and redecoration (including repairing plasterwork), was followed by the re-roofing of the nave. Tindall initially proposed two redecoration schemes: the 'forbidding grey and beige' colour scheme of the nave was either to be replaced with a vibrant bright and colourful scheme (similar to that he carried out during the restoration of the former Victoria Hall on Castlehill – now The Hub), or what he called 'the plain white' option. Paint analysis had identified that the original Burn interior had been painted in a stone-effect covering, now too dark for modern tastes,

and the congregation opted for the off-white option although the chancel was returned to its original blue colour, and gilding was applied. As part of the re-plastering a new boss, moulded as a portrait of the rector, Rev. John Armes (who had succeeded Chamberlain in 1998), was subtly inserted in the porch entrance, and finally, pews were removed from the west end to allow more circulation space for the ever-increasing numbers of visitors.

The success of St John's' programme of diversification, and its increasing status as a visitor attraction, has in turn necessitated further expansion. In 2005, LDN architects were commissioned to produce a scheme to refurbish and extend the hall, provide new office space, a lift (to improve disabled access), and improve the lower terrace spaces. No final scheme has been agreed to date. In the past, the architectural development of St John's displayed, on the one hand, a respect for its unique landscape context and neo-Gothic forms, whilst on the other, attempting to meet the changing needs of its congregation. This delicate, successful balance is a tradition worth maintaining.

May 2004 view of St John's congregation.
© St John's Episcopal Church

Unexecuted 1835 perspective design for a memorial to Sir Walter Scott by W H Playfair. The towering obelisk to Walter Scott has St John's delicate neo-Gothic as its picturesque setting. SC466199

Selective Bibliography

St John's Episcopal Church

Published

E W M Balfour-Melville, *A Short History of the Church of St John the Evangelist*, 1959

J F Mitchell, *Edinburgh Monumental Inscriptions (Pre 1855): St John's Episcopal Churchyard, Buccleuch Burial Ground, Jewish Burial Ground & Quaker Burial Ground*, 2003, Scottish Genealogy Society, Volume 3

St John's Chapel, History and Statement of Accounts, 1815–37, bound volume, National Archives of Scotland

St John's Magazine, 1928–39

St John's: The Church of St John the Evangelist, Edinburgh, 1996

G F Terry, *Memorials of the Church of St John the Evangelist*, Edinburgh, 1911

Un-published

'Church of St John The Evangelist, Edinburgh, 175th Anniversary Talks on History, Architecture and Restoration of St John's Church', typed transactions, March 1993, St John's Church Archive

Fettercairn Papers (correspondence of Sir William Forbes of Pitsligo and his family), MS/4796/220, National Library of Scotland

L Hodgson, 'St John's', 1818–1965', unpublished typed manuscript (held by author)

St John's information leaflets, which include: *The History of the Scottish Episcopal Church*; *A walk round the Church of St John the Evangelist*; *Architecture* (J Jameson, 2004); *The Organ* (S Doughty, 2005); *Monuments* (A Mitchell, 2000); and *Windows* (L Hodgson, 2000), St John's Church Archive

D Walker, manuscript of reception speech to mark the completion of restoration programme at St John's, 18 March 1993, St John's Church Archive

Architecture and Art

J Ballantine, *A Short History of Church Stained Glass: A lecture delivered before the Scottish Ecclesiological Society, 9th December, 1911*, Edinburgh, 1911

J Ballantine, *A Treatise on Painted Glass*, Edinburgh, 1845

H Colvin, *Biographical Dictionary of British Architects*, 1600–1840, London, 1978

J M Cunliffe, 'Some Observations on an Early 19th Century Architectural Practice', in *Edinburgh Architectural Research*, Vol. 4, 1977

Dictionary of Scottish Architects, 2006, online at www.codexgeo.co.uk

R Dixon and S Muthesius, *Victorian Architecture*, London, 1985 (second edition)

M Donnelly, *Scotland's Stained Glass*, 1997

R Fawcett, *Scottish Medieval Churches*, Edinburgh, 2002

J Gifford, C McWilliam and D Walker, *Edinburgh, The Buildings of Scotland*, London, 1984

M Glendinning, A Mackechnie and R MacInnes, *A History of Scottish Architecture*, Edinburgh, 1994

M Glendinning and A Darragh, S*t Mary's Episcopal Cathedral, Edinburgh: A Short History and Guide*, RCAHMS, 2003

M Glendinning and A Mackechnie, *Scottish Architecture*, London, 2004

M J Lewis, *The Gothic Revival*, London, 2002

I G Lindsay, *The Cathedrals of Scotland*, 1926

C McKean, *Edinburgh, An Illustrated Architectural Guide*, Edinburgh, 1992

S McKinstry, *Rowand Anderson, The Premier Architect of Scotland*, Edinburgh, 1991

A Maclean, 'The Scottish Episcopal Church and the Ecclesiological Movement, 1840–60', in Caledonia Gothica, Pugin and the Gothic Revival in *Scotland, Architectural Heritage VIII*, 1996

A W N Pugin, *Contrasts*, London, 1841 (second edition)

T Rickman, *An Attempt to Discriminate the Styles of Architecture in England from the Conquest to the Reformation*, London, 1848 (fifth edition)

S Rush, 'John Knox would have kicked this out of the window: Edinburgh and the Early Stained Glass Revival' in *The Journal of Stained Glass*, Vol. XXX, 2006

G Stamp, 'Introduction', in *Caledonia Gothica, Pugin and the Gothic Revival in Scotland, Architectural Heritage VIII*, 1996

St Giles' Cathedral: Stained Glass Windows, 2000

J Thomas, *Watercolours by R W Billings (1813–74)*, RCAHMS, 1996

D Walker, 'William Burn's Fashionable Functionalism' in *RIBA Journal*, October 1990

D Walker, 'The Rhind Lectures 1990–1: a synopsis, The Revival of Medieval and Early Renaissance architecture in Scotland, 1745–1930', in *Proceedings of the Society of Antiquaries of Scotland*, 121, 1991

D Walker, 'William Burn (1789–1870)' in *Oxford Dictionary of National Biography*, Oxford, 2004–7

Church History and Biographies

Dictionary of National Biography, 1917

F Goldie, *A Short History of the Episcopal Church in Scotland*, 1976

D Wright, D Lachman and D Meek (eds), *Dictionary of Scottish Church History and Theology*, Edinburgh, 1993

Oxford Dictionary of National Biography, Oxford, 2004–7

T Veitch, *The Story of St Paul's and St George's Church*, 1958

A Maclean, 'Episcopalians' in C Maclean and K Veitch (eds) *Religion, A Compendium of Scottish Ethnology, Volume 12*, Edinburgh, 2006

Index

Note: page references in *italic* refer to illustrations

Royal
Commission on the
Ancient and
Historical
Monuments of
Scotland

100 years

St J⊕hn's

St John's Episcopal Church Edinburgh

Situated at the westernmost entrance to Princes Street, St John's Episcopal Church enjoys the enviable picturesque backdrop of Edinburgh Castle and the Old Town. It stands today (despite later additions) much as it was when first designed almost 200 years ago – a celebrated architectural monument and place of worship in the heart of Scotland's capital.

This richly illustrated book examines the history and architectural development of St John's from the early 19th century to the present day. It attempts to re-evaluate St John's architectural significance and legacy, whilst exploring the broader religious and cultural impact of the church on the Christian life of Edinburgh's New Town. St John's interior was unprecedented in Scotland in 1818, and it was the first of the new Gothic towers and spires that formed the 19th century 'Romantic Edinburgh' cityscape. Its pioneering commemorative stained glass, and neo-Gothic military memorials, enhance its overall unique value as a treasured 19th century Gothic ensemble.

ISBN 978-1-902419-51-0

9 781902 419510